# Jewish Dharma

# Jewish Dharma

A GUIDE TO
THE PRACTICE OF
JUDAISM AND ZEN

## BRENDA SHOSHANNA

Da Capo
∞
LIFE
LONG

A Member of the Perseus Books Group
*New York*

Copyright © 2008 by Brenda Shoshanna

Designed by Pauline Brown
Set in 10.75 point Goudy by the Perseus Books Group

Cataloging-in-Publication data for this book is available from the Library of Congress.

First Da Capo Press edition 2008
ISBN-13 978–1–6009–4043–9

Published by Da Capo Press
A Member of the Perseus Books Group
www.dacapopress.com

Da Capo Press books are available at special discounts for bulk purchases in the United States by corporations, institutions, and other organizations. For more information, please contact the Special Markets Department at the Perseus Books Group, 2300 Chestnut Street, Suite 200, Philadelphia, PA 19103, or call (800) 810-4145, extension 5000, or e-mail special.markets@perseusbooks.com.

1 2 3 4 5 6 7 8 9—10 09 08 07

This book is dedicated to
my great teachers in both Judaism and Zen—
Soen Nakagawa Roshi, whose wonderful free spirit,
filled with joy and playfulness, along with deep
dedication to dharma, set my feet along this path, and
Eido Shimano Roshi, whose incredible devotion to
practice and endurance allowed both of us to persist
and grow through all kinds of joyous and difficult times.

The book is also dedicated to my incredible brother,
Dovid Myerson, who has been my chevrusa, my Torah
learning partner, and dearest friend throughout my life.
All of these years we have discussed, debated, and deeply
encountered the issues dealt with here. He has
been a constant support and true inspiration, a deeply
observant Jew who is also a totally free spirit, filled with
wisdom and love for all.

And a special dedication to my grandfather, Moshe Snitofsky,
whose love of God, Torah, life, and all people was never
ending. I always see him singing in his sukkah
under the grape vines, shining with joy.

# CONTENTS

# Contents

# SPECIAL THANKS

I WISH TO THANK so many people who have been deeply instrumental in the birth of this book, my many wonderful teachers and guides along the path, particularly Lubavitch Rebbe, Jillalamudi Mother, Rabbi Dovid Bleich, Judy Bleich, Rabbi Joseph Gelberman, Joko Beck, Sogen Yamakawa Roshi, Kyudo Roshi, Lester Levenson, Rabbi Ephraim Wolf.

I also wish to thank my editor, Matthew Lore, for his wonderful guidance, and my family for unfailing support: Gerry, Melissa, Abram, Joshua, Yana, Adam, Noah, Zoe, Remy, Jake, Maya, Zachary, Louis, and Mildred Myerson and Dora Snitofsky.

I particularly thank the supporting, ongoing members of the Mishkan, our center for Jewish and Zen practice, for their dedication, inspiration, and participation in putting these two practices together, particularly Haskell Fleishaker, Richard Schiffman, Bernie Starr, and Michael James Creeley.

And special thanks to my many dear Zen friends and those who have practiced with me throughout the years, particularly Peter Gamby, Chinshu Scott Young, Seigan Ed Glassing, Fay Tabakman, Bill Solomon, Stuart Schwartz, Jeff Asbell, Ernest Castaldo, Michael Klein, Ralph Zeitlin, Zensho Martin Hara, Yukon Grody, Aiho Shimano, Larry Crane, Jacques Van Engel, Constantin Wickenburg, and Jacques Amsellem.

*Special Thanks*

Beyond all I thank God for allowing me to make this offering. May it be a blessing to all and give honor to the true spirit of heaven.

# INTRODUCTION

*Teach us to care and not to care*
*Teach us to sit still.*
— T.S. ELIOT

AS A LONG-TERM ZEN student and practicing Jew raised in Borough Park, Brooklyn, who has been unable to let go of either practice, I have struggled for many years with what appear to be the completely different teachings of Zen and Judaism. Gripped by these two powerful, ancient practices, I have finally come to realize that despite all logic, each is essential to the other. Zen practice deepens Jewish experience, and helps one understand what authentic Jewish spiritual practice is; Jewish practice provides the warmth and humanity that can get lost in the Zen way.

Fortunately, I am not alone in this conundrum. There are an estimated 1 million Jewish Buddhists "in the United States today ("JuBus," as they are often called)—a number which is rapidly growing. Since the 1950s, Jews around the world have slowly turned to Buddhist practice—so much so that today, of the 3 million Buddhist practitioners in the United States, nearly one third of them are Jewish. What is the connection between Judaism and Zen? How do they shed light upon one another?

Today a great spiritual hunger is surfacing as many seek comfort, support, and meaning in a world that has spun out of control. There are endless paths to take, yet most modern Jews and non-Jews as well have little knowledge of what authentic Jewish practice and authentic Zen practice actually are. When we look at Judaism today, we see a mass of conflicting customs, traditions, and rituals. Many Jews are leaving Judaism, feeling rejected by it, or thinking that the practice is too complex or disconnected from the realities of today's world. Many have become spokespeople and teachers for the spiritual practices of the East, including Zen.

However, Zen practice, improperly understood, can lead to unexpected difficulties. Zen students need the warmth, grounding, balance, and life perspective that Judaism provides. And clearly, Zen is offering Jews something that is deeply needed as well. What is this? Do Jews need to leave their own religion to embrace Zen? Or is Zen able to make their own traditions come alive to them in new, important ways?

In a sense, Judaism and Zen represent two opposite ends of a continuum: Zen is based on radical freedom, individuality, being in the present, and nonattachment. Judaism comes rooted in the family relationships, love, prayer to a Higher Power, and the injunction to hold on and remember. A Jewish heart is warm, giving, human, devoted to family and friends, and filled with longing for the well-being of all. A Zen eye is fresh, direct, spontaneous, planted in the present moment. It is unencumbered by ideas, beliefs, tradition, hopes, or expectations. These practices are like two wings of a bird: both are needed for it to fly.

This book will show you how Zen and Jewish practice illuminate, challenge, and enrich each other. You will see how each tradition addresses the primal questions that drive your life and provide keys for finding answers to the personal struggles you face today. Each chapter deals with different life issues, and shows how both Jewish and Zen practices can assist in handling them. Specific guidelines and exercises are included.

The need to combine zazen with Jewish practice and teachings of Torah always felt very important to me, and I am aware of many individuals, both Jewish and Christian, who wish to practice their original religion in a way that feels healing and congruent for them. The practice of zazen creates an atmosphere of love, acceptance, respect, clarity, kindness— and not only illuminates one's original teachings, but provides a deeper experience of them. And conversely, one's religion of origin brings a dimension to zazen practice that is beneficial, grounding it in the reality of who you are and where you've come from.

It is too easy to lose sight of the true purpose of any practice we do. Even with the best intentions, blind obedience to forms, obsession, and group pressure to conform can and do lead many astray. Anger, judgmental attitudes, and domination can easily replace the kindness, generosity, and wisdom that are at the heart of all true practice. Practicing both Zen and Judaism together is a protection against this. It creates a balance which clears away the weeds and allows your understanding to sharpen and your life to bloom. In order to experience this, it is important to know what each practice consists of, and then to try it for yourself.

In my home we have a zendo that is dedicated to combining Jewish and Zen practices in an authentic way. Both Jews and non-Jews participate; it has been very meaningful for all. We do zazen practice as usual on regular days, but when we gather on Sabbath afternoon include Torah study, prayer, and blessings as well. In preparation for each Jewish holiday we hold a three-day retreat that goes on for eight hours each day. We dedicate the retreat to deepening our connection to God and to that specific holiday. During the retreat we do zazen for many hours, and when the time comes for chanting, chant Hebrew prayers (usually Avinu Malkeinu). Each day we offer blessings, prayers, and dedications, either out loud or silently, depending on the individual's wish. When the time comes to hear a talk, we study the teachings of Torah and the sages regarding that particular holiday. We may also combine Zen teachings on a particular point as well. During our Rosh Hashanah retreat, while sitting in zazen, we listen to the shofar blow. At Chanukah, during zazen, one member rises, says the blessings in Hebrew, and lights the candles. As we do zazen, the candles flicker upon us all. For Shavuous, along with zazen, we spend extra hours in Torah study. For each holiday, we include particular observances related to that holiday, and also enjoy delicious holiday food.

This combination of zazen and Jewish practice has wonderful effects. As we sit in zazen concentration grows, stray thoughts lessen, defensiveness dissolves, the heart opens. This deeply uplifts and enhances the study, prayers and blessings. After the study or prayers, we return to zazen and deeply digest all that has gone on. This is an ongoing process and exploration, where all can claim the totality of who they are, honor where they've come from, and turn to their original teachings more deeply, live and see them now, in a fresh, vital, and authentic way.

Ultimately, you cannot taste the real fruits of a practice until and unless you take some of it on and apply it in your life. As you embark upon a practice that includes both Zen and Jewish practice, you will see the ways in which they cross-fertilize one another, how Zen practice deepens and clarifies your understanding of Jewish teachings and how it enhances the experience of prayer. You will also see how the warmth, wisdom, and deep sensitivity of Torah study can place your Zen practice in a broader context and allow it to more easily be integrated into everyday life. The book is intended for Jews, non-Jews, Zen students, and all engaged in other practices who desire to expand their wisdom or enrich their lives. It will speak to all individuals who are seeking understanding and meaning, and wish to live a life grounded in authentic faith.

## Cautions

Today there are different points of view within the Jewish denominations about what practice truly consists of. This book attempts to provide an introduction to essential Jewish practices based on Torah and halacha (Jewish laws), as well as to the practice and principles of Zen. I recognize that readers of this book come to it from various backgrounds and perspectives. Certain practices will feel natural and inviting, while others may seem dissonant, or impossible to take on. That is fine. Each practice is not for every person. In the Torah itself each person is encouraged to find the particular portions and practices that are meant for them. An ancient Rabbi, Rabbi Baer of Radoshitz, made this a primary point in his teachings. He said it is impossible to tell men what way they should take. Instead they should find that that speaks to them, that which they can integrate and which is uplifting. For one the way to serve God is through the teachings, for another through prayer, another for another through fasting, and still another through eating. Everyone should carefully observe what way his or her heart draws them to and then choose this way with their entire strength.

If you fall into guilt, pressure, or condemnation of yourself or anyone else, you have lost the purpose of both practices, which is to bless, awaken, and heal the entire world.

# CHAPTER 1

# Jewish Prayer and the Practice of Zazen

*Be still and know that I am God.*
—TORAH

IWAS BORN INTO an Orthodox Jewish family in Borough Park, Brooklyn. My grandpa, grandma, mother, father, sister, brother, and I lived together in a three-family green and white house with benches outside, a garden with irises, and a big cherry tree in front sheltering us all. Our synagogue, Shomrei Emunah, was on the corner of the block and my yeshiva, Shalomis, was located in a small building a couple of blocks away. There were two other synagogues on our block as well, but my grandpa could always be found at the one on the corner, singing, studying, helping anyone who came his way. To him nothing mattered but the word of God.

My grandma and grandpa lived downstairs. My family lived on the second floor, and we gave the third floor apartment to those who escaped from the Nazi camps. At night I took food upstairs for them and left it at their door. Sometimes I could hear them inside crying, asking God what they'd done wrong. When I heard them crying, I would run downstairs to my grandpa and ask, "Grandpa, why did this all happen? What did we do wrong?"

"One day God will tell you why everything happens," he whispered. "When you merit it, when you're strong."

Then I ran to my grandma, who was cleaning in her kitchen. "Grandma, why did all this happen? What did we do wrong?"

"Normal girls don't have these kinds of questions. Just stay and work with me in the kitchen, cut the vegetables, sweep the floor. What else are you looking for?"

My grandmother was huge and strict, with a stiff brown wig, and had a hard time with me. "What kind of a girl came into this family? Stop asking questions, stop chasing after your grandfather, running to shul. It's not allowed. Don't listen to anything your mother tells you. She is lost in dreams. Stay here with me and work in the kitchen. That's the only way." So, for a lot of the time, I worked at her side in her white tile kitchen, chopping carrots with a blunt knife.

Everybody in the family had a different opinion about the right way, about what God wanted. My grandma and grandpa, devout Jews—Hasids—kept everything strictly; they were pillars of the religious world. My grandmother served God by preparing meals for Shabbos (the Sabbath). Her door was always open; anyone who was hungry could come and eat. My grandpa sang to God constantly, no matter what he was doing, night and day. My other grandpa, my father's father, who was also a Hasid, sat upstairs silently in our apartment on Shabbos in his long black coat. All day long he studied Torah and hardly spoke, except to warn us not to gossip. My mother loved to tell stories and wrote beautiful poems that she would read to anyone who would listen, even though she knew it wasn't allowed. My father, a lawyer who was not religious, said he loved God by working hard and taking care of his family. He walked down the street, in full view, without a yarmulke on and would never set foot in the synagogues.

And me, I had a lot of questions: what was the true way, what did God really want from us, what difference it made if we did things differently, and why people who were serving God with all of their hearts had trouble living together in the same house. When Shabbos came, there was no place I could rest. My father wouldn't let me stay upstairs in the apartment because I was too religious and drove him crazy. He refused to have a daughter like that. My grandmother wouldn't let me in to her apartment downstairs, because I wasn't religious enough and didn't give her any rest.

So, I sat on the steps between the first and second floors wondering where, if anywhere, I belonged, and what God really wanted of me. Afraid to do anything that might break the Shabbos, I would just spend hours sitting quietly, wondering. Although I didn't know it at the time, I later realized that this could be regarded as my first experience of Zen meditation, or zazen—sitting quietly, not moving, nowhere to go, nothing to lean on, taking a question, and entering deeply into my own heart and mind, waiting for a reply. Those years on the steps were precious, though I didn't realize it at the time.

## Drawing Spiritual Nourishment
## Through Jewish Prayer

Times of loneliness, confusion, doubt, or separation come for a powerful reason—so we can stop our usual way of being and discover where true strength, connection, and understanding lie. These difficult times are actually a blessing, removing us from preoccupation with externals and inviting us to embark on a journey into the heart and meaning of our lives.

Prayer, or *tefilah*, is the heartbeat of Jewish practice. It is a powerful way to dissolve loneliness and confusion by turning to something greater than yourself, opening your heart, and learning to see with new eyes. Prayers are a communication link to God, a way to develop a relationship. They affect not only the world within but also the world around you. Prayers for others can heal and uplift them; prayers for mercy draw forth merciful, loving energies. It is very important to be aware of what you pray for—what your thoughts, desires, and words express. As you pray for healing for others, healing energy will return to you as well. Forgiveness is always the greatest prayer. It heals the world and lifts the one who offers it. As you forgive others, you are forgiven.

Observant Jews gather together to pray twice a day, morning and early evening, in a minyan, a group of at least ten men. The community is essential, not only in lifting the prayers and strengthening them but in reminding us that we are not alone. Being present for others in the minyan and helping them in times of need is a form of prayer as well. (Women are always welcome but are exempted from time-bound mitzvot, due to the demands of raising children.)

As the men pray together in the minyan, scripted prayers are said. These prayers were carefully designed, composed thousands of years ago by the Rabbis of the Great Assembly and are chanted today exactly as they were centuries ago. As this happens, ancient experiences, memories, and miracles become available right now.

The precise time the communal prayers are offered is very important, as these prayers create a connection between Jews scattered throughout the world. Wherever they may be, no matter how distant from one another or in what culture when they are praying, the language, timing, and posture are the same. As they are chanting the same words at the same moment, there is no separation. Each prayer lends power to the others. In the midst of their prayers, all are one.

The time prayers are offered is also important because these prayers combine with and affect the different physical, emotional, and spiritual energies that arise throughout the day and night. For example, morning prayers set the tone of the day, opening the heart and mind to a new vista; evening prayers create a protective shield against the depression and darkness that arise at night. In this way we are guided and supported through the changes we go through as the day passes by.

I learned about prayers in Borough Park, Brooklyn, where they surrounded everything that went on. The whole world I lived in was about twelve square blocks large. The narrow streets were lined by thin trees that struggled for air. Everyone on these streets lived together, with their entire families and beloved Rabbis. There was nowhere else in the world you had to go. Everything you needed was right here.

Each block had at least one or two synagogues on it. Most were only narrow rooms inside people's homes. In the middle of the room stood long wooden tables strewn with Bibles and prayer books where the men sat for hours, praying, learning, and repenting their sins. There was even a synagogue behind Ruthie's grocery store, where the men could smell delicious, fresh sour pickles as they begged God to save the entire world.

Evening came slowly in Borough Park, not like anywhere else in the world. As the light started to fade, a hush descended as the men prepared for mincha and maariv, the late afternoon and evening prayers. It was almost as if the stones on the pavements were waiting to hear the ancient melodies. One by one the doors on the block opened and men dressed in black came scurrying out flying in all directions to be on time at the synagogues.

"We praise God, no matter what," my grandmother Devorah told me over and over, "in good times and bad. There is nothing that happens that is not God's will for us."

I swallowed hard whenever she said that. "Everything is God's will for us, Grandma? Even what happened in the war?"

"Even that. Even that."

## The Many Kinds of Jewish Prayer

In Judaism, there are many ways to praise God, many kinds of prayers—communal prayers, prayers from the heart, and spontaneous prayers that arise suddenly from the depths of your being. There is *rinar*, a shout of exaltation or pain that arises suddenly in a moment of deep experience; *shagoyen*, a wild, wandering prayer, like music; *hallel*, a more intense form of praise, from which the word "hallelujah" arises. *Zemer* is a chant, *shira*, a song, *nechomus*, a prayer for consolation. There are prayers of petition, praise, blessings; prayers for healing, consolation; prayers of remembrance. One of the most important functions of prayer is to place you in a state of praise and thankfulness, no matter what is going on. The Wisdom of the Fathers, a sacred Jewish text, says it clearly, "Who is a Jew? He who praises God continually."

Communal prayers are like a voyage that takes you from one experience to the next. You start by blessing and praising God for creating the abundant goodness and beauty in the physical world. You give thanks for the fruit of the trees, earth under your feet, stars, water, trees, food. In Judaism, the physical world is never rejected, but hallowed and sanctified. Everything encountered is part of creation and exists for you to love, praise, and uplift.

Judaism teaches that everything in the natural world is a miraculous process. The physical and spiritual are completely intertwined. Prayer sanctifies the natural life processes, and faith is necessary for livelihood. In fact, prayers are discussed in depth in the agricultural section of the Talmud because prayers are like seeds. Not only do you have to plant them in special ways at special times, but you must learn how to reap the harvest as well.

Prayer is also referred to as mist. The Talmud says, "A mist goes up to heaven." Just like mist, prayers go up and activate the flow of spiritual sustenance. This sustenance is then called down into your life and the life of others through prayer. Ultimately the work of Jewish practice and prayer is to elevate and bless the entire world.

## "Come to Me Directly"

After giving thanks for the physical world, communal prayers turn to human life and God's intervention in the universe. God is never impersonal or distant but rather deeply involved in all of creation and is an active, living partner in our lives. The Torah states, "Come to me directly, not to man whose breath is in his nostrils." We are told not to go to God through a messenger, angel, relationship, or fantasy. Our help will not be found there. Instead, we are to enter into direct relationship with the Eternal and call on God for everything. It has even been said that God created all the difficulties in the world so that we would come to him in prayer and discover where our true sustenance lies. No matter what you are facing, your daily dialogue with God through prayer will provide a way through difficulty and times of sorrow.

In order to begin, it is not necessary to know Hebrew, study Torah, grow up in an observant home, or even be Jewish. You can pray in any language, at any place, at any moment. Prayer from the heart is always the most powerful and direct. Many stories tell of learned men praying and praying in the synagogue, while the doors of heaven remained closed. Yet when one simple person sitting in the back row dressed poorly called out sincerely with his entire heart, the doors opened and blessings were brought down for all. A true longing to reach out, an open heart, and a sincere mind cannot be ignored.

Although this may sound unbelievable or anthropomorphic to many, it is useful to stop for a moment and realize that you cannot really know the truth of this matter until you try it for yourself. The power, effectiveness, and reality of prayer cannot be figured out intellectually. They operate beyond the conscious mind. In order to discover the power of prayer, you must try it and see what happens, not only to events in your life but to the way you begin to feel. True prayer not only ascends above but breaks the heart open, crushes the false sense of self, and allows light and understanding to shine in.

There are many ways to begin. Some are listed below in the section on practice. The simplest (and perhaps most powerful way) is just to open your mouth and heart and speak out. You may have no sense of God or the Absolute. That need not stop you. Just call out to the universe any way you can—speak, chant, sing, write, paint, garden. If one way does not suit you, try another. In doing so you will discover Who it is you are connecting to. Prayer is the natural need and call of the heart. A heart that cannot pray is often closed, numb, and hurting. Prayer opens the heart. It soothes, heals, instructs, and connects you with wisdom and kindness from above and from within. When prayer is truly, sincerely offered, the Torah teaches that there is always a response. It cannot be otherwise.

This beautiful teaching not only builds faith but refers to the deeper fact that when you offer prayer sincerely and wholeheartedly it affects and changes you. When you reach within to that which is most meaningful, your consciousness alters. From deep within, new feelings, insights, and responses come. Many studies show that praying for the sick significantly impacts their healing. They receive the energy of love and good wishes sent forth to them and this enhances their recovery. In the same manner, true prayer impacts both you and those around you.

## Zazen Practice:
## Returning to Yourself

Few have experienced a world like Borough Park, where life centers around prayer, night and day. Many would not want to. Yet all people need to bring a vital experience of aliveness, connection, and meaning into their lives. Zen practice cuts through all religions, denominations, and systems of thought. In my view, Zen is not a religion but a practice that enhances and enlightens all activities. This practice can be done anywhere, by anyone, at any time, in any condition of body and mind. Zazen reaches into the very core of your being and brings forth that which is healthy, sincere, creative, and real; it heals loneliness and separation.

I found out about Zen in an odd way. When I was fifteen years old, my history teacher approached me in the classroom and handed me something folded in a brown paper bag. Take this home and open it," he said. "It's just for you. Don't show anyone."

Excited and frightened, I took the package home and opened it when I was alone in my room. In it was a thin book, *On Zen*, by D. T. Suzuki.

I devoured the book immediately, and even though I had no idea what any of it meant, I felt great joy as I read. This is it, I kept thinking, delighted, with no idea why I was so happy at last. For years I held on to that book, reading it again and again, taking it everywhere I went. When people asked what it was about, I said, "I have no idea." And I didn't; I just couldn't stop reading the koans. I loved every one of them. For years I didn't realize there was a practice, how to find it, or where to go. It took me seventeen years to find the zendo, and an entirely new, unexpected life began.

In many ways Zen meditation, or zazen, seems to be the opposite of Jewish prayer. In this practice you do not pray for help daily; in fact you do not pray for help at all. In zazen you sit, back straight, legs crossed, eyes down, facing the wall. You do not speak, reach out, touch, or listen to the troubles of others. You do not offer consolation or turn to others for support. In fact, what you thought of as support is taken away. If others are having trouble on the cushion, experiencing sorrow or pain, you do not interfere. Their experience is precious and they are now being given the opportunity to face it fully. The support you offer is silent and profound, just sitting strongly beside them, facing your own experience and not moving.

As you engage in this practice, you discover that there is nothing you need to lean on. Everything you need is right here, sitting on your own cushion. Just as you are, you are complete and whole. The only problem is you do not realize it. Your life and mind are so cluttered you are so attached to it that which has no value, and are constantly seeking more.

Zazen is a core daily practice, much like daily Jewish prayer. It focuses the mind and heart, allows you to gather your scattered energy and get in touch with your essential self. As you practice daily, your life becomes rooted in its original source. Gradually your perceptions of life alter and you become able to live a life of simplicity, sincerity, and truth. And when you become simple, focused, and open, every action turns into a prayer.

Soen Roshi, former abbot of Ryutakaji monastery in Japan and great twentieth-century Zen Master, used to say that when most of us want to see beauty in a room, we bring in fancy paintings, furniture, precious objects. In Zen, when you want to see beauty in a room, you take everything out, one thing after another. When the room is empty, you can see its original nature. Its beauty shines by itself.

In Zen practice you do the same. You take everything out of your life that causes clutter, static, confusion, greed. You take out plush furniture and people to lean on. As you do this, you naturally find your own inner balance and strength.

Usually, most of us live our lives in the opposite manner, seeking strength, comfort, support, from everything and everyone. But the more we search, cling, and hunger, the worse our suffering becomes. Soon we are slaves to the external world, easily manipulated by anyone or anything that offers a temporary salve or cure.

Zazen practice rejects all of us. It teaches not to lean, not to weaken yourself and others this way. The entire basis of zazen practice is to cut the dependent mind. It insists that we stop tossing and turning, stop clinging to objects, and turn instead to the very source of our life.

But what is this *source* of life? How is it different from *God*, who is constantly called out to in Jewish prayer? Some say that Zen has no God, is coldly indifferent, and rejects life. But for many the opposite is true. Because I was taught there was only one way to find God, for many years I could not understand why the more I did zazen, the deeper my experience of God became. On the surface it seemed contradictory but in practice, it was the fact. I don't know if I ever would have been able to go back to synagogue without the deep sense of well-being and acceptance that developed as a result of zazen. The more I sat, the deeper my trust in life grew, and as my concentration deepened, the more I was able to let go of extraneous thoughts.

After a while, during zazen I began to remember the old prayers I had loved so much as a child. They started softly but over time became more persistent, eventually causing me to return. Later on in synagogue, I was able to pray with deeper intention *(kavannah)*, concentrate more fully, not be so distracted by others, and experience the prayers and teachings in an entirely a different way.

Perhaps this is even more surprising, because in Zen practice, there is not a specific concept or image of God, of what or who you are turning to. In zazen you do not linger in ideas, pictures, and concepts. A well-known Zen saying reminds us that painted cakes do not satisfy hunger. If you are starving and go to a restaurant and sit there studying the menu, it will not fill you up. Instead, you must order the food, eat it, and digest it for yourself in order to be satisfied. Similarly, sitting in zazen, rather than thinking about the meaning of life, you directly absorb all that life has brought to you. This is not a rejection of God.

It is simply a refusal to name, define, or limit what happens. Every person's experience is allowed to arise as it will. For each it is different. Whatever it is called or named, as practice deepens, that which is vital and joyous surfaces and turns a person's life around. It brings strength, wisdom, and endless compassion. As this happens, not only do loneliness and separation dissolve naturally, but lives become hallowed and strong.

## Zen Practice and
## the One Who Walks Alone

Jewish practice insists on being together. In Jewish practice there is constant interaction with others. It is hard to find a second to be alone. Even if you enter into deep prayer in the midst of the congregation, the minute it is over, others are greeting you, shaking your hand, asking how the family is doing.

Zen practice asks, Who is the *one* who walks alone, who is the solitary one? This question is fundamental not only in Zen practice but in our lives. How many lives are run by the fear of being alone, how few are at ease by themselves, how often we seek the company of others compulsively, to escape what's going on in our lives.

Zen practice values being alone, facing ourselves, standing on our own two feet. In Zen the question of the solitary one has often been misunderstood. It does not point to an antisocial individual who withdraws from life, but to a person who journeys deep within his or her own nature, addressing the primal questions of life and responding according to their individual spirit and wisdom.

A great tenth-century Zen Master, Zuigan Gen Osho, dealt deeply with the question of being alone and not depending on others. While he was alone, he called to himself every day, "Master!"

Then he answered, "Yes sir!"

"Be wide awake!" he would call back.

"Yes sir!"

"Do not be deceived by others."

"No, I won't be."

From deep within one voice called and the other voice answered. Zen students ask, Who was the one who was calling? Who was the one who answered? Who is the one who deceives others? Who is the one who is wide awake? This is the great prayer of Zen practice, finding this one—not being caught by delusions or wasting our lives as a make-believe person.

From the Zen view, we spend most of our lives deluded, expend our energies daily on things that have no importance at all. We do not see clearly that which causes difficulty and that which brings true contentment. Often we trust others, only to find that our trust is misplaced.

Zen practice is a rigorous journey to self-trust. During this journey it is necessary to walk on your own feet, breathe through your own nostrils, and open your eyes wide. You are not to walk in the footsteps of another. You are not to hold on to long cherished beliefs indiscriminately. Instead, you awaken and directly confront the matter of life and death. Where are you from? Where are you going? And what happens in between? Above all, you are not to be deceived by others, but to find out for yourself.

## Become a Person Who Cannot Be Deceived

Someone asked Yamakawa Roshi, a modern-day Zen Master at Shogen-ji monastery in Japan, how he could avoid being deceived and betrayed.

Yamakwa Roshi answered, "Become a person who cannot be deceived."

But how can we become so clear and strong that life no longer deceives or betrays us? How we can become real? I had no idea how to do this until I discovered Zen teachings.

I arrived at the zendo the place where zazen is taught and practiced, on a Thursday evening in March and received beginner's instruction, how to sit, how to walk. I barely knew where I was, except that, as I walked with others along the bare wooden floors, I knew that I had returned home. I couldn't stay away. A few days later, I went on a Tuesday afternoon and found myself sitting on a cushion next to a monk from Japan who eventually became my Zen Master. I could barely sit; I was very new. There were just a few of us in the zendo. Suddenly he spoke out, punctuating the silence in a deep, resonant voice that entered every pore. "In this practice, you are not being asked to believe anything. All you have to do is come here, sit down, and find out for yourself."

I was stunned, thrilled, astonished. Every inch of my body came alive. Was it possible? Here was the spot I had been deprived of: a place to come and find the truth for myself.

That afternoon was only the beginning. I have sat beside him and others in the zendo year after year. I still sit. Years passed, shocks happened, joy, sorrow, disappointments. But no matter what, I keep returning. I have to find out for myself. As my Zen Master and I sat together, many times I wondered what it was that brought a tough, samurai Zen Master from Japan to end up sitting next to a restless Jew from Brooklyn, who sat on her cushion and cried. It must have been very hard for him too. Both of us displaced from our culture; both of us passionate about zazen.

"Stop crying," he would growl, sitting strongly and fiercely beside me. I would just cry more. No matter how much he shouted at me and demanded silence, it took years of sitting for the crying to end. Once the crying ended, so did his shouting. In the beginning of practice, I would arrive at the zendo at 5:00 A.M., almost every day, for morning service. The zendo would be mostly empty, except for a few students and Japanese monks. My Zen Master would be sitting at the front of the row, wrapped in his robes, doing zazen so profound you could feel it miles around. The zazen drew me; it healed, soothed, and awakened all that was waiting within. So, even though many times he scowled at me, yelled, and tried to get rid of me over and over, the very next day I would return. I couldn't wait to hear the morning gong ring.

In the early days after going to the zendo for several weeks, everyone became a member. After a couple of months of going every day, excited, I made an appointment to see the Zen Master and become a member too. It was our first time to talk. After early morning zazen, I nervously climbed the stairs to his meeting room on the second floor. He sat formally in his black robes, on his cushion at a low wooden table with two teacups on it. I bowed, entered the room, sat down on a cushion opposite him. He very carefully offered me a cup of tea.

I received the tea and, together, we drank.

After we finished and put our teacups down, he paused and looked at me.

"Yes?"

"I've been sitting here for two months now."

He looked a bit surprised. "You have?"

I was shocked. I had sat next to him every morning. How could he not know I was there?

"Of course. I've been here every morning."

"Really?"

There was a long pause. "I want to become a member."

He stared at me. "Why?"

I was speechless.

"What difference does it make, member or nonmember?" he said.

"Absolutely none."

"Exactly."

Our interview was done.

The next day, I came back to sit anyway.

Zazen practice is not about belonging. It is not about being noticed or accepted. Even though you sit next to others, you must find out what it means to be alone and experience your aloneness through and through. As you do, you may realize that aloneness is not loneliness. In fact, it is the opposite.

There are many ways of learning to stand on your own. Several months after I asked to become a member, Soen Roshi, my Zen Master's teacher, came from Japan to spend time with us all. One morning, as we were all having tea upstairs, some students were talking about being members. Although I said nothing, Soen Roshi looked at me, his eyes twinkling.

"I am a member of the universe," he whispered. "How about you?"

## Finding God at the Kitchen Table

In Jewish practice, you must belong. You are not allowed to isolate yourself. Over and over you are told that it is not good to be alone. In fact, there is a painful assumption in many communities that there is something wrong with you if you are alone. The place to find God is not away from life, on a mountaintop or in personal seclusion, but at the kitchen table—among family, friends, food, discussion. The experience of God is never separate from life and never separates you from those you care about or from your daily life. Coming to the kitchen table is like coming to a minyan; different individuals lend their particular spirits, gifts, strengths, and also blemishes and weaknesses. As you live and interact with others, you become balanced and whole. In Jewish practice, a continual community is available; there is a continual kitchen to go to—if you fit in. This question of fitting in, or not, to the community has driven many Jews away. But joining together in community, a willingness to share your spirit and also to receive from another, is itself a form of prayer. It is relinquishing self-centered obsession and opening to whatever and whomever life brings along.

## Gathering Together:
## The Minyan

Gathering together in a minyan is central to Jewish practice. Individuals return twice a day not only to stand before God with their own personal cares, but also to be there for one another, to be conscious of and responsive to what their neighbors are going through. As they pray, they are accountable not only for themselves, but for each other. Each person in the minyan takes a part of the other's burdens and offers his or her strength in return.

When a minyan is not present, the kaddish, the traditional Jewish prayer for the dead, cannot be said. This prayer requires the strength of ten to lift the mourner, lift the prayer, and lift the spirit of the departed. It is even said that the holy spirit (*shechinah*), rests on a minyan. Another reason women are not required to pray in a minyan is because they are considered to naturally carry the holy spirit with them. Even though many think going to a minyan is simply a routine, traditional matter, it's much more than that. When you pray with a minyan, unexpected, powerful events and changes often take place.

My father died three years after I started Zen practice, and I was estranged from Judaism at that time. The grief, pain, and shock of his sudden loss were extremely difficult to bear. Night after night I had dreams of him; I tossed in bed dreaming that he was lost, upset, and in great pain. During the day, the feelings from those dreams hung on. I strongly felt that he was not at rest, and neither was I. No matter how much I sat in the zendo, peace about this did not come, and the dreams continued.

Then a Jewish holiday came when yahrzeit candles for the departed were lit and special prayers offered. I went to synagogue for the first time in a long time, to pray for my father. When I heard the ancient melodies, I was suddenly swept away with emotion, tears fell, my body swayed on its own, and prayers enveloped my entire self. Terrified, I started to run out of the sanctuary. Then over my shoulder, I saw a fat man chasing after me. Alarmed, I thought he wanted to kick me out, that he knew I somehow didn't belong. I ran faster. Gasping, he caught up with me at the door.

Backed into a corner, I turned and faced him. "What do you want?"

"The Rabbi told me to come after you," he breathed heavily. "He said you should come to the minyan every day."

Stunned, I pulled away, slipped out the door, and ran all the way home.

But in a few weeks, there I was, at the minyan night and day. Though I was the only one in the woman's section to come regularly, I said the kaddish prayers for my father, faithfully, every morning and evening for an entire year. As I did, my dreams subsided; my pain eased. My father and I rested. And I loved being there so much, I stayed on for another year.

Some are regulars in the minyans. Others come for certain occasions, to celebrate a birth or marriage, or to pray for help in time of illness or distress. Some come for a drink of schnapps, company, charity, a business deal, connections, or to come in out of the cold. All are to be welcomed. The minyan is a little world where nothing is left out; everything is elevated in prayer. Those who are regulars in the minyan are constantly available and aware of all that is going on not only in the minyan but in the community at large. They are privileged to witness the never ending cycle of birth, marriage, business, illness, recovery, death—times of joy and times of loss. Whatever is needed by those in the community, the regulars are always there.

The minyan I attended always included Chaim, a little man in his late seventies with twinkling eyes. He had escaped from Russia and now his whole life revolved around the minyan. In the morning he made sure cookies and schnapps were there. In the evenings, he made sure the doors were open on time and the siddurs (prayer books) were ready. Even when he was younger and ran his candy store, the last thing he did before he went to sleep at night was make his calls, to make sure they'd have a minyan the next day. Especially when it was icy out or snowing. "God forbid we don't have enough for the minyan and someone needs to say kaddish. I couldn't sleep all night if that happened," he said.

## Seclusion and Meditation

Seclusion does not have to mean separation. Times of deep seclusion and meditation can allow us to return to life and be there fully, carrying great gifts in our hands. As zazen deepens, many students begin to attend sesshins—intensive training periods where the students leave their normal routines, go away, or are otherwise secluded with others who are attending. This is a time to concentrate on practice. External demands are removed, distractions are eliminated, and conditions are perfected in order to use the time to journey within. This period of seclusion is considered vital for intensifying practice and breaking through barriers along the way. After sesshin, you take what you have learned and bring it back to daily life.

Jewish practice also has a long history of meditation and seclusion, though of a different kind. In Jewish practice the sages of old used to sit for one hour, pray for an hour, and then sit for another hour. When they sat, they became silent, still, concentrated and empty, much like zazen. The first hour of sitting was a preparation for prayer, preparation to meet "the King." The next hour was spent praying. After that they sat for another hour to absorb the effects of their prayers and wait for a reply. They did this three times a day. Right in the middle of their lives they were secluded. When asked how they could have possibly taken care of their physical needs, they said that when they did this, God provided everything.

Rebbe Nachman of Breslov, a great eighteenth-century Jewish sage who breathed new life into the Hasidim and still has thousands of disciples today, taught his disciples to seclude themselves in prayer, calling this *hitbodedut*. He told his students to go under a tree at midnight and call out to their Creator whatever was in their heart. If they could not do that, they were to go under the covers every night and have a good talk. During this they were to make a reckoning. What were they doing with their lives? How were they spending their time? He said that if they made God the judge over everything they were doing, they would be able to rid themselves of all fears and worries. All this could be achieved through *hitbodedut*, secluded prayer.

Seclusion of all kinds, practiced both in Zen and Judaism, is ultimately for the purpose of developing strength, clarity, and a deeper connection with Self or God. After that you return to daily life, present, available, able to truly see what is going on and what is needed in return. So many times you receive replies to prayers or new possibilities or guidance, but your life is so busy, your mind so confused, that it is difficult to see what is in front of your eyes. All true practice teaches us how to open our eyes.

When we do not receive what we want through prayer, or when difficult times come along, it is easy to become discouraged or lose faith. This is due to not understanding the true nature of prayer. We take a step and are tested when our prayer is turned down. Are we going to continue only when things go our way, like small children who pack up their toys and leave if they don't get what they want?

True prayer teaches how to build a strong heart and character, how to remain constant during adversity. As we remain constant in prayer, we grow to see that all experiences are needed, no matter how difficult they may seem. If we never felt pain, we could not feel joy. Without times of difficulty, we could not rejoice in times of gladness. When we numb ourselves and refuse to feel sorrow, we also become numb to the goodness of life.

A man was drowning in a boat and begged God to save him. Someone arrived to help him bail out the water, but the man paid no attention to him, just continued his fervent pleas. As the boat continued to sink, another boat pulled up and extended a lifesaver. "Leave your sinking boat," the person cried. But the drowning man had shut his eyes to everything except his cries to God and the way he expected God to save him. He drowned and went to face his Maker. When he stood before God, he complained, "I cried to you, as you required. I was a good man. I did all you wanted of me. Why did you let me perish?"

"I didn't let you perish," came the reply. "Didn't I send you boats to save you? It was you who let yourself drown. You never opened your eyes."

## Guidelines to the Practice of Jewish Prayer

### TURNING POINTS

*Discovering Your Daily Prayer*

To enter the world of prayer, decide to spend a certain amount of time each day praying. You can spend this time simply being silent and communing with whatever brings you peace. Or you can spend the time in nature, or quietly with a loved one. Just spending time together in silence is a wonderful form of union and prayer.

It is also possible to try to speak to God (or your higher self) in your own words. Let your thoughts flow. Speak silently or out loud. It is also fine to spend this time in contemplation, going over what is or is not meaningful in your life. The important point is to set aside some time and space in the midst of your busy world and dedicate it to the Infinite. Work, service, or creative endeavors done with mindful reverence for life are forms of prayer as well.

Others may prefer more formal prayer. Get a prayer book. Find something that touches you. It can be a prayer of praise, blessing, a prayer of thankfulness after meals, or perhaps some psalms (*tehillim*). Sometimes just one sentence is enough. Take it in and dwell on it. Or perhaps you may be drawn to do more. It is not a question of how much is done, but the sincerity you bring to it and the meaning it brings to you. Try to do this every day. As you do so, the prayers themselves will guide you what to do and where to go.

The Shema is the essential Jewish prayer in all the services. It is a simple, powerful declaration of basic faith: "Hear, O Israel, the Lord our God the Lord is One." Over the centuries, as Jews have faced death or danger, this prayer was on their lips and in their hearts. The Shema is so profound because it is a total declaration of both faith in God and complete oneness. You are being reminded that ultimately there is no separation between any aspect of life. It is considered important to say this every day. If you want to say it in Hebrew, the transliteration is "Shema, Yisroel, Adonai Elohaynu, Adonai Echod." Some say it over and over, to keep themselves constantly aware of the presence of God.

Some may want to pray with others or increase the time spent. Others will want to create their own prayers. Each way is wonderful. If you want to pray with others, try out different synagogues. Each one is different. Find one that suits you and makes you feel welcome.

## Guidelines to the Practice of Zazen

### START WITH SILENCE

Even if you do not wish to do zazen practice, there are many ways to stop endless activities, distractions, and thoughts, and give yourself time to be quiet and simple. It is as simple as stopping. Simply sit down, turn off the TV, radio, or mp3 player, put aside to-do lists and other responsibilities, and just be for a few minutes. Stop talking. Practice silence. Allow yourself time to come to balance and to rest.

Feel the whole universe with you, feel the wind on your face, your body on the chair, your breath coming and going; take a moment to appreciate the enormity of who you are and what is before you, day by day. As you do this more and more frequently, not only will the world change around you, not only will natural thankfulness arise, but the meaning and fruits of your labors will become increasingly clear.

### PRACTICING ZAZEN

To practice zazen, get a cushion on the floor (you can also sit in a chair if it is too difficult to sit on a cushion), straighten your spine, and cross your legs (half or full lotus is good if possible; if not, just cross-legged). Keep your head straight, eyes slightly open, and look down ahead of you. With your hands in front of your belly button, put your left hand in your right hand with thumbs touching lightly. Put your mind (attention) in your lower abdomen *(hara)* and begin by counting your natural breath from one to ten.

When you get to ten, go back to one and start again. Don't breathe in any special way. Let a long breath be long and a short breath be short. Once the sitting begins, *do not move.* Sit for as long as you can. In the beginning, ten or fifteen minutes is fine. When thoughts come, just notice the thoughts and go back to the breath. When you lose count due to distractions, just go back and start at one again. The important point is to not move at all. Usually when we are uncomfortable, we try to fix or change whatever causes disturbance. An itch comes and we scratch. Here we just sit with whatever comes and simply experience it. Then we go back to the breath.

Happiness comes, pain comes, pleasure comes, and they go. As we sit, we allow whatever comes to come and whatever goes to go. Do this every day, for as long as you are able. (Even ten minutes a day makes a big difference.) Regularity is very important. As your practice deepens, your zazen will guide you on what to do next. At some point sitting with others is very helpful and there are many Zen centers all over the country. But today just start with the first breath. Actually, in Zen practice, every breath is the first breath.

CHAPTER 2

# Seeking Understanding: Torah Study and Koan Practice

*A scholar who is not inside*
*as he is outside is no scholar.*
—TALMUD

THERE ARE SO MANY mysteries, paradoxes, and inscrutable questions we face daily that cannot begin to be addressed by analytical, rational thought. Many people struggle with how to live their lives, what events mean, what actions to take and what not to. There is so much that cannot be truly known. And yet today, all doors are open. Endless streams of spiritual and religious thought are available with so many different teachers and gurus that it is hard to know what to believe.

How do you know the right path to take? How do you find true understanding? How can you sift through lies and delusions, distinguish the sage from the trickster? These questions haunt many who wander from one practice to another. They also haunt some who are in the grip of a tradition that may not

speak to them, that seems to have lost its relevance and aliveness. Ultimately there are no simple answers.

Both Judaism and Zen have unique means of deepening
your ability to cope with that which is unknowable, paradoxi-
cal, or difficult to understand. Each practice will take you on a
different journey that overlaps suddenly in unexpected ways.
Both practices ask you to dedicate your life and energies to
finding and living from the ultimate truth.

## Seeking and Finding

### HOLD FERVENTLY TO THE PAST

In both Jewish and Zen practice, individuals are fervently
seeking. Jews constantly seek to increase their knowledge of
and attachment to the divine. Zen students seek truth, realization, awakening. In fact, these are two sides of the same hand.
In Torah a promise is made, "If you seek me truly you will find
me." What exactly will be found, and how is a Jew to seek?
Torah gives specific steps to take to not only to find the truth
of existence but to become able to live a life of deep purpose,
meaning, and fulfillment.

At first glance, Jewish and Zen practice offer *seemingly* opposed directions. The Torah declares, "These teachings are for
all generations." Do not follow passing customs and fashions
but hold on to the ways of old. If you connect to that which is
timeless, it will prevent you from getting caught in passing
fads, confused teachings, and customs, which can cause years
of harm and waste. By understanding and following the teachings of the past, by honoring and following ancient sages, your
life will bear rich fruit.

## LEAVE THE PAST BEHIND

The life of a Zen practitioner also bears rich fruit, but Zen proclaims that the past is gone, the future not here, and the present appears for an instant. You are to leave the past behind and not dwell on the future. Instead, stay planted in the moment fully, right here, right now. You must not walk in anyone else's footsteps; reject imitation. There cannot be real knowledge unless there are real people. Unless you become real, all your so-called knowledge will only be secondhand imitation. You must have the courage to be who you are. In fact, unless you wake up and become able to do this, you are only a ghost, a person who never really came to life. As a great Zen poet, Basho, put it, "Do not seek to follow in the footsteps of the men of old; seek what they sought."

In striving to arrive at ultimate truth, Judaism insists on using the mind intensively; analytical thinking is honed to the finest extent. The Zen student finds ultimate truth by not lingering in ideas or concepts; koan practice is designed to bypass the "thinking mind." Zen practice is based on radical freedom, living from the mind that is boundless. Jewish practice is based on deep obedience and surrender to the word of God, as passed down through the centuries. But these are just differing forms of practice; the ultimate truth is the ultimate truth.

What happens to someone who tries to practice both? After my father died, I went to the minyan twice a day to say kaddish for him. I was also deeply involved in Zen practice. I couldn't let either go. There were days when one practice deepened the other; there were other days when I felt as though I were being pulled apart between the two. Neither my Zen Master nor my Rabbi had the least idea how to deal with this, so I wrote a letter to a teacher in India, Bhagwan Osho, whose books I had been reading and loving, describing my plight.

To my surprise, he replied quickly. "Don't try to figure anything out. Leave no traces, do both practices completely—100 percent. Just stay away from politics wherever you go." That helped greatly: not only did I not have to make a choice, but also felt he was leading me to discover the deeper connection between both worlds.

Whenever we embark on a spiritual practice, it is easy to find glaring differences, not only between our practice and others, but contradictions within our practice as well. These differences and contradictions often become obstacles that force us to grow if we are to overcome them and continue forward. Many leave their religion of origin or other spiritual practices when these obstacles, contradictions, and disappointments arise. Some cannot reconcile the inner contradictions in their practice; others notice glaring disparities between the teachings they follow and the behavior of the clergy, and feel this invalidates all they have been taught.

In this regard, it's extremely important to stand on your own two feet, take the teachings into your own hands, and live them with all your heart. Zen practice encourages students to go beyond paradoxes and attachment to a teacher. A famous Zen saying instructs us, "Do not put a head on your head. What's wrong with your own head anyway?"

As Master Zuigan, introduced in Chapter 1, showed us, you must not be deceived by others, but have the power to grapple with the teachings directly and awaken your own heart and mind.

Looked at from the outside, the fruits of Zen practice and the way we arrive at them seem to be in opposition. Although as practice ripens, we develop individuality, uniqueness, and spontaneity, during training we must maintain a strict posture in zazen, sit long hours, be disciplined, not move, obey the Zen Master, go through a great deal to dissolve ego, arrogance, and pride. What has this got to do with finding our freedom, being who we are?

Similarly, Jewish practice also can point in potentially confusing directions. Analytical thinking is honed as Jewish practitioners spend hour after hour studying the Torah and Talmud and analyzing each little word, looking for connections and meanings, learning to see things fully and clearly. And yet they must obey the word of God, listen to their teachers, keep the mitzvot, and honor many customs that may not seem relevant today. In order to reconcile these contradictions, it is helpful to realize that all practice works on several fronts simultaneously. When you seek true understanding, you must work with both your head and your heart. By surrendering your momentary personal wishes, dreams, thoughts, and impulses, and allowing yourself to be guided by larger directives, you are dissolving the defensive and impulsive parts of yourself that cause so much pain. You surrender the part of yourself that thinks it knows everything and insists on having your own way. In Zen this is called ego. In Judaism it is called the evil inclination (*aetza hura*). It is the part of ourselves that criticizes, obstructs, and sabotages our best efforts. When we are told to obey or to follow something larger than ourselves, we are working on our heart. Judaism also calls it the soul; Zen calls it Buddha nature.

Judaism and Zen work with both head and heart so that practitioners learn to take what they learn and make it into their flesh and bones. In Torah study, you use your mind to think, learn, and grow, and at the same time obey that which is beyond your understanding. Zen practice provides koans to occupy the thinking mind while you sit in zazen. These koans force you to come up against your usual ways of knowing and functioning and to see how useless they may be.

Both practices have inherent dangers. When you cling to the past, fear may develop, or an unwillingness to look outside your own world; you may begin to think others are wrong and inadequate, to be shunned and avoided. A fundamental rejection of life can take place. This is actually the opposite of true Torah teachings. The true Rebbes never rejected the world or the nations. In fact, the great Hasidic masters used to take the songs of drunkards in taverns and convert them into prayers.

The Zen way can also present snares if not practiced properly. It can lead to blind self-involvement or encourage the idealization of or attachment to a teacher. You can inadvertently create a world apart and become isolated. This too is contrary to Zen teachings, which constantly return you to your very life. You may be tempted to go from one teacher to another, tasting and comparing. However, this can scatter your energies, increase doubt, and multiply misgivings.

When you seek true understanding, whatever practice you engage in, you must persist through times of pain, loss, confusion, and disappointment, times when you can't understand what's going on. These are often the times when there is the greatest opportunity to grow. If you run away, nothing happens. Ultimately you must be able to endure and find out for yourself.

Seeking and finding in both Zen and Judaism require persistence—the ability to absorb disappointment and disillusionment. Each practice calls you to experience the essence of life, forgo distractions, focus your energies, let go of pride, and develop true compassion. Zen is called the middle way, and Torah presents a life of balance. Each calls to a new way of life.

## The Way of Torah

The Tanakh (Bible) includes the five books of Moses (Torah) and many other volumes, including Psalms, prophets, laws, commentaries, and allegories. Collectively it describes the relationship between God and the world. It includes all aspects of existence; nothing is too small or insignificant to be considered. It explores communication, business dealings, agriculture, love, marriage, and sex, down to the most minute details. The main goal of Torah is to make a home for God in this world. The Lubavitch Rebbe, the head of the Chabad Hasidim who brought Judaism to Jews all over the world, said, "Torah is not on the mountains or far away. It is here on earth, in your own hands and lives to fulfill." You follow the teachings about when to pay your workers, what blessings to say, how to safeguard your roof, how to treat your family, what the best time for lovemaking is. This is not to take away freedom, but to put you into contact with that which is highest and best for all.

In Torah there is no separation between the divine and the reality of everyday life. One mirrors the other, and in each the other can be found. Given our limited sensibilities, we cannot truly be aware of all the repercussions of our choices and actions. The Torah therefore acts as a guide and protection, both for us and the world at large. Torah study is considered to be one of the most important mitzvot. As we study and fulfill the teachings, the smallest act becomes consecrated to the service of God and therefore heightened and filled with significance. This is the meaning of the "living God."

Growing up, I learned about Torah study through Reb Bershky, a rabbi who lived two doors down from the house I grew up in. He had a small synagogue in his home, where he sat at a long wooden table, studying Torah all day long. He was a very tall, thin man who hardly ate and sat alone all day wrapped in his black satin coat studying the word of God. Nothing else interested him. I would go to his alley and peek in the window and see that he spent every moment deep inside the sacred pages that were spread out on the table before him. No matter how many pages, Reb Bershky read them all; he drank in every word. Not only that, but the words drank him in. If you looked closely, you could find no separation between them. I used to think, thank God for Reb Bershky. If he is here praying with us, it is possible that God will take pity and save the entire world.

Even when I was little, I kept dreaming of running away. The world outside called me. I wanted to get on the bus and take a good look at the neighborhoods all around. This, of course, was strictly forbidden. A girl's place was at home. When the wish was too strong, I'd go speak to Reb Bershky, who would always let me come in and sit at his side.

"I don't know what I'd do without you here, Reb Bershky," I'd say.

"It's not me, we're all perfect," he'd barely whisper. Beyond that, he'd keep still. His words pierced my heart in a way they had no right to. I would just sit there beside him, waiting for more.

Finally he'd look up at me and say, "We can see God in every moment, if we only learn how to open our eyes."

"My eyes are open."

"Not far enough yet."

A few rays from the late afternoon sun would shine through his tiny window, and the lace curtains would stir gently, playing with the sun and brushing against the glass of tea that stood on the corner of his table. Most of the time he didn't drink it. The tea would stand there until it got cold. But he didn't need tea. He didn't need anything. He didn't get hungry or thirsty. Me, I got hungry and thirsty, I got lively, restless, curious. The world around me pulled me. I wanted to get up and run right into it.

Just when I was thinking that, Reb Bershky would look up at me and say, "Where exactly do you want to go?"

I didn't have to say a word out loud. He could hear everything everyone was thinking, even the thoughts they had not yet had. Looking deep into those ancient pages of Talmud, the whole world was spread out before him clearly—both the world within and the world outside.

"Forgive me please, Reb Bershky, but I want to fly the whole world over. My mother said if you're alive, you're meant to fly."

There was pain on his face when I said that. Such a thing could not be imagined.

He sat up tall then, a huge tree unfolding, and said, "When we sit in one place, quietly learning, God holds us tightly in his arms. Then there isn't any place we aren't flying. Sit quietly in God's arms and then someday, when you are ready, you will be shown everything."

You can still find scholars like Reb Bershky studying in hidden rooms. But whoever studies Torah on any level is considered to be in direct touch with God. Whether or not you are aware of it, as you study you bring down spiritual nourishment, not only for you but for others as well.

There are many ways of studying Torah, many ways of living it and many reasons for Torah study. On one level, you study in order to know which mitzvot to perform (what actions to take and when). On another level, you are being taught how to think; how to make distinctions and comparisons, understand the true nature of the world you live in and how to function in it.

A yeshiva is a place where Torah is studied. When you enter you receive a partner (*chevruta*). Together you take one phrase, one law, or one teaching and chew on it relentlessly. You study every commentary the rabbis made on it throughout the ages; you look at it from every vantage point until it becomes your entire being, occupies your total thought. Before long you realize that the rational aspect of this phrase is simply one small portion of its greater meaning.

Sometimes the stories you encounter in Torah seem obvious, but you must look deeper. You then turn to allegorical interpretations and secrets embedded within words and images. You visualize different letters and use them as doors to contemplate deeper meanings. Torah study shows how to break limited, restricted thinking. Torah study becomes a means of altering your consciousness, a form of meditation. For Torah students, the entire world exists in layers, hidden by veils. As they study, the veils part and true understanding arises. The more deeply they study, the more clearly they can see beneath the great mystery life presents. The more committed they are, not only to study but to actually practice what they learn, the more the Torah reveals itself and the more their lives are guided and protected in all kinds of ways.

Torah study is also a form of purification; it calms the mind and burns out inner negativity. And here is where Jewish practice and Zen suddenly intersect. In order to truly get to the heart of Torah, it is not so important what you *do*, but who you *are*. Torah requires inner change, simplifies your life, creates humility.

So many people today think that just by sitting down and reading Kabbalah they can understand its meaning. This notion is mistaken because the secrets are not contained in words. The secrets are revealed when one is free of arrogance, selfishness, anger, and pride. The Kabbalah itself tells you not to study Kabbalah until you are forty because Jewish practice focuses so strongly on not leaving the world, on being grounded, mature, able to fulfill your responsibilities here. (These days some Rabbis feel this restriction has been lifted. Others do not.) There is always the danger in Kabbalah of getting carried away, focusing too much on other dimensions as an escape from life. Once there were three rabbis studying Kabbalah's secrets. In the process all three entered *pardes* (heaven): one died, the other went crazy, and one returned to the world. The highest way to study Torah is *l'shmo,* just for the sake of studying it, for the privilege of being connected to God. Intention is vital. It's important to make a blessing before you start to study, indicating that you are now fulfilling the mitzvah of Torah study.

## Koan Practice: What Is It?

Life presents endless conflicts, contradictions, and paradoxes, which we usually try to solve logically, analytically. Rarely do we succeed. Koan practice is a way of breaking through paradox and confusion and finding a new kind of understanding and a way to respond. Koans bypass the rational mind. As you work on a koan, you must throw away words, concepts, and ideas, which can hypnotize, delude, and lead astray. You begin to see that the answer to paradox, conflict, and contradiction does not reside in books or scriptures, but is hidden within the self.

Koans are an essential part of Zen practice. What is a koan? It is a question given to you by the Zen Master when your practice has reached a certain depth. This question cannot be answered logically. At first the question may even seem absurd. Yet it is not absurd; it is vital. You must bring an answer. If you do not or cannot, your very life is at stake. A well-known koan is: "Show me your original face before your parents were born." The rational mind cannot answer it, and yet another part of you can. Koan study wakes this part up. When the concept-forming activities of mind are quieted, the deeper wisdom emerges. This wisdom is spontaneous, intuitive, appropriate to the moment; it heals and empowers. Many believe there is a "right" answer to a koan. Books have been published presenting so-called solutions. However, if you presented what you read in a book to any real Zen teacher, you would be dismissed from the room immediately. Such an answer would never be approved. Somebody else's answer belongs to that person and can never be right for you. The basis of koan practice is neither figuring out an answer nor imitating someone else. It is not what you "know" but who you "are"—

who you become as a result of your struggle with your koan, the effect it has on you. An answer to a koan that is passed for one person could easily be turned down for someone else. When you are told to find your "original face before your parents were born," no one else can find it for you.

Learning how to work on koans is a process that takes time. By sitting with koans, going to dokusan (interview with the Zen Master), and presenting an answer and failing time and again, you find out for yourself. My Zen Master always said, "The best encouragement is no encouragement. It is your own effort and struggle that make you clear, real, and strong."

However, we are all trained to imitate others and figure out solutions to inscrutable problems intellectually. Inevitably, when you start to work with your koan, you will approach it as you would any other problem in life. You'll try to analyze it, strategize about it, and find fancy answers for the Zen Master's approval. However, every time you see the master in interview and bring something contrived, you'll be dismissed, time and again.

The next time you go to see him, you will try something else and fail again. Old habits die hard. Failure after failure piles up fast. These failures are actually good for you; the more the better. It's possible to struggle with one koan for years. Though this is often humiliating, it is your ego that is being dismantled. As time passes and failures accumulate, pride diminishes and you become dissatisfied with a secondhand response. As this goes on, the part of you grows that is able to live a straightforward life. I worked on one koan for over three years. Year after year, time after time, I went to dokusan and brought something cooked up. The moment I said it, my Zen Master rang the bell, indicating the interview was done.

Discouragement mounted. I must be crazy, I thought. Or maybe it's him? Maybe he just hates me and doesn't want to say yes to anything? Maybe both of us are crazy? What am I doing here anyway? There's nothing I'll ever be able to do right.

Discouraged or not, I was determined to solve this. In those days, my Zen Master offered dokusan every Wednesday night, and I went time and again. One night when the bell rang for dokusan, though I had nothing new to offer, I trudged upstairs to wait in line. Finally it was my turn. I rang the bell to announce I was coming and then flew up the next flight of steps, opened the door to the dokusan room, bowed, and blurted out loudly, "I hate my koan; I hate myself."

My Zen Master smiled. "Now we're getting somewhere," he said."

Koan study is a lengthy process that includes times of discouragement and frustration. Everyone wants to run away and I did, many times. For years, I was the great escape artist. Even though it was forbidden, I would escape during sesshin, much to my Zen Master's dismay. When I returned over and over during these years, he never once said a word to me about it. We just picked up where we had left off.

Maybe he knew that wherever I ran, the unanswered koan would keep dragging me back. Maybe he was relieved that I was gone. But it didn't matter. As I kept working with the koan, old fictions about my life and my self dissolved. Slowly I began to come to dokusan quieter and emptier than before. My false, fantasizing mind was fading. One day, as I was sitting on the dokusan line, I noticed I was no longer looking for his approval or for a way to keep from being kicked out of his room.

This particular day I had nothing much to say, but when I went upstairs to dokusan, he seemed unusually pleased. "Now you must redouble your efforts," he insisted. "Work on the koan continually, night and day. Okay?"

"Okay."

For no reason at all I got excited. The koan dug in further. I began to dream about it night after night. It became both a constant companion and a thorn in my side. At odd moments, it focused me completely, announcing, "Here I am."

Here is a wonderful instruction about working with koans: "When you are doing zazen sit as though you were a mother hen sitting on her nest, keeping her eggs warm. The mother hen doesn't move or leave the nest alone. When they are ready to be born, the chicks burst through all by themselves."

The koan is no different. One day it bursts open. It is shocking and profoundly altering. The minute you walk into the dokusan room, the master knows.

But that is not the end of the story or of practice. It is actually the beginning. Now zazen goes deeper. Now you sit more, not less. Old problems, sorrows, questions still come up in many ways, but you hold them differently. There is more to do, more koans to grapple with. You may even be given the old one you thought you had passed and fail it once again. The biggest difference is that you are no longer fragmented into so many warring aspects, you're not trying to figure the odds so much, hoping for success and approval, or searching for some ultimate answer that will miraculously stop all your pain. If it rains, you let it rain. If it doesn't, you walk in the sun.

## Jewish Practice:
## Do and You Will See

In one sense Jewish laws (halachas) are Jewish koans. Koan study is not so different from the hours of study that Torah students go through in the yeshiva, wrestling with and dwelling on one phrase or law until its deeper meaning opens up. Observing the laws is a kind of koan practice as well, because the true nature and effect of these actions cannot be grasped logically but must be encountered through experiencing them directly for yourself.

During the past two hundred years, these Jewish laws have been disputed by different denominations, some laws accepted, some rejected, others altered. Nevertheless, the laws are the bedrock on which discussion is based. Some hold that these laws are divinely given; others feel that they are human creations and can be altered, depending on the times and circumstances. Others approach the entire Torah as literature or mythology. How do we know which is true? The Torah has a fine suggestion: "Do and you will see."

Follow the law and see what happens for yourself. (This does not mean follow every law. Do what you can.) This matter is so vast that it is beyond thinking over or figuring out. Like the Zen koan, these laws are beyond rational explanation. Some are clear and obvious; others seem strange. No matter how they may seem, like Zen koans, the laws are something one *does*, not something one *thinks about*. As you start to follow the laws, life changes. Insights, strength, wisdom, and solutions to problems often come unexpectedly on their own.

Of course the law can feel like a straitjacket, keeping freedom away. The question of how to find real freedom, though, is the underpinning of both Zen and Jewish practice. Most think they find freedom by doing what they like and running wherever they want to go. It's easy to run away from study, from laws, from koans, and from life itself. Dreams of all kinds beckon. This great question, of how we truly break the constraints that bind and harm us and find true freedom, can take many years to answer. It is a universal koan.

When a great Rabbi was asked what was more important, study or action, he answered action. Unless you put your study into action, your study is not fulfilled. And you cannot know what action to take unless you study. A bird needs two wings to fly.

## EVERYDAY LIFE KOANS

So often we turn life circumstances into problems, as if they were something to be conquered and changed. When you view the circumstance as a koan, however, it is no longer a problem but something that has taken place. All you need do is be present for it and allow yourself to experience all facets of it. The important aspect of this is not going into your head with dreams about what could have been, fantasies about what will be, or explanations and interpretations that away take the reality of your experience. Just be with all of it as it arises day by day. When you treat problems as koans in this way, deeper understanding and the right course of action will be revealed.

For example, let's say someone you care for ends the relationship and you can't accept it or understand why. Not only are you angry, sad, lonely, and upset, but you're also confused about why this happened. Your sense of self is shaken, as is your ability to trust. Normally, you might start trying to figure this out, blame yourself or your partner, go over what happened endlessly, dream of ways to make the person love you again, or strategize about protecting yourself from this ever happening in the future. Your ability to go forward is halted. Obsession can easily take hold here, along with other negative responses.

When you view this situation as a koan, however, you do not indulge in what I just described. Instead, to begin, you accept the situation as it is, including all your painful feelings and thoughts about it. You do not try to fight it, change it, understand it, regulate it, gain sympathy from others about it, or blame yourself or the other—you simply experience it fully. When a wave of pain comes up about it, you stop and let that be, feel it without commenting on it, just let it wash over you. You don't try to hide from what you are feeling or distract yourself with other activities. Even though you may not be seated on a cushion, you are sitting with the situation, welcoming it, saying okay. This is not passivity but an active process that takes great strength and courage, and will yield wonderful results.

As you treat problems as koans, not only the circumstance will change but you will change as well. You will begin to see it differently, have new feelings, perceptions, and insights about it. Rather than feeling vulnerable and fearing relationships in the future, working in this way will not only give you strength to go on but provide a fresh way of being in the future with whomever or whatever comes along.

As you live with koans in this manner you no longer live in a black-and-white world but one that is full of possibility. You will be able to respond spontaneously and appropriately to whatever the moment brings.

## Guidelines for Jewish Practice

### DAILY TORAH STUDY:
### ALLOCATE A TIME EACH DAY

The way into Torah study is simple. Allocate a short time each day to stop and read a small part of the weekly portion (parshah). The Torah is divided into weekly portions, and there are many editions that contain wonderful commentaries on each page (Rashi and Hirsch are two of the best known). These can be purchased at all Jewish bookstores and online. Read a section of the weekly portion and then look below at the interpretations. As you do a little day by day, your interest may grow along with your momentum, and your understanding will deepen.

You can also read any of the other books in the Bible—the prophets, Psalms, or commentaries, whatever speaks to you.

If possible, go to a class at a local synagogue or place of Jewish study. There are also many fine discussions and classes available online. The important point is to get started and allow your study to show you where to go next.

### GUIDELINES FOR TORAH STUDY

There are important guidelines for Torah study that are taken directly from the Torah itself and can be followed beneficially in many other areas of life as well.

#### *Set a Fixed Time for Learning*

To begin, it is helpful to set aside time each day to study, even a few minutes. This time will bless, nourish, and uplift all the other hours of the day.

### *Do Not Make a Spade of Torah Study*

Do not "use" the Torah for personal ends. Do not study to achieve recognition, wealth, or personal desires. In days of old the greatest Torah sages worked hard all day at simple labor, for example, as a blacksmith putting shoes on horses, and then at the end of the day sat under a tree and studied with a few others. No money passed hands.

### *Constantly Ponder What You've Learned*

This may seem impossible in the present day, given the demands of life and the nature of relationships. However, we still can try to bring Torah teachings into the different aspects of our lives. The Lubavitch Rebbe said that great things were demanded of previous generations, but in this generation, even a small change of a habit means a great deal. Beyond that, Torah teachings are all related to your daily activities. Whatever you are doing, you can apply a Torah teaching to it. If someone is irritating you, see how this can be turned into a mitzvah; find a way to keep your peace. (More about this later.) It is interesting to think about what Torah would say about the circumstances facing you each day.

### *Take Stock of Yourself*

It is important to take time regularly to look at your thoughts, deeds, and words and take stock of yourself. In this way you can correct errors, acknowledge growth, and turn your footsteps in a direction that is beneficial for both you and others. These words are written in Torah and were famously proclaimed by Socrates, who said that the unexamined life is not worth living.

### *Apply What You Learn*

This point is crucial. The heart of Torah study is practical and is to be made real in everyday life. In fact, whatever happens in your life can be seen as an opportunity to apply the teachings. This gives a totally new take on life. Nothing can happen that is bad or unacceptable; you are simply being given an opportunity to grow and apply what you have learned. In this respect Torah is the teaching and life is the opportunity to learn it in one's flesh and bones.

## Cautions

Every gift comes with the possibility of being misunderstood or misused. This is even more true when the gift is of a greater magnitude, when it can become a blessing. Therefore, it is crucial to recognize the fact that the practices, teachings, and customs in Torah are not meant to be used against anyone, though this can happen. The danger of feeling inadequate, guilty, excluded, or compulsive is always present. It is easy to overlook what you have already accomplished and focus on what is left to do, to feel overwhelmed and feel like a failure. Although a fundamental practice in Torah is to judge others favorably, this is sometimes forgotten. Some judge themselves or others relentlessly if they do not follow the teachings. Others praise themselves unnecessarily for following certain behaviors, without going deeper and attaining true kindness or integrity. In order to separate the wheat from the chaff, to come to the living spirit, you must constantly note and carefully avoid these dangers. Particularly because it is so all encompassing, the practice of Torah must be taken on with care, respect, health, and compassion. You must keep the larger purpose in mind—to heal, uplift, and bless the entire world, including yourself.

# Guidelines
# for Zen Practice

### KOAN STUDY

Although you may not have a teacher to work with at this time, you can still begin to view situations in your life as koans. Are you involved in a difficult, painful relationship that seems to have no way out? Is there a rough business situation, a painful recurring pattern? Are you dealing with illness or disappointment?

Take these as your koan. Stop trying to figure them out, strategize, solve, manipulate, or change them. Give up fighting the situation, judging it, or running away. Welcome it completely. If you do zazen, sit with it on your cushion, let it permeate your life, experience it as it is without judging or fighting it. As you do this, unexpected solutions and possibilities will appear, and you will change as well.

If you wish to formally enter koan practice, it is important to find a Zen center and a teacher to guide you. Sometimes you will immediately recognize the right place or person to work with. Or you may find it useful to explore; go from to Zen center to Zen center to see where you are drawn to practice. Sometimes, after you start sitting, the teacher comes later, on his own. Finding the teacher is itself a koan. There is a saying that when the student is ready, the teacher appears. Remember, the ultimate teacher is your own zazen.

## Cautions

Koan practice, when not done properly, can become an obsession, a way of blocking out life and disregarding important issues that need to be handled. You can begin to feel as though you are doing the most important thing possible and may not take the time needed to attend to what is in front of your eyes. The practice can also lead to excessive dependency on a teacher, the feeling that someone else can give or withhold validation. Although true koan practice helps dislodge these feelings, it is possible to get stuck. It is also important to realize that even though you may solve all your koans, there is no reason for pride, or feeling as though you are special in some way. This is simply a form of "Zen sickness." Ultimately, life itself is the true koan, and unless you can respond to life fully and freely, practice has gone awry.

# CHAPTER 3

# Disciplining Yourself: Mitzvot and Mindfulness

*Purify your heart to serve me sincerely.*
—TORAH

U SUALLY WE THINK OF discipline as something negative, a yoke around our necks that curtails freedom. We all want to be free and today there is a huge desire to create new traditions, do as we wish, pick and choose our own structures and rules. Along with exhilaration and growth, this process can also bring confusion, loss of anchors, and dislocation. A sense of boundaries and meaning can be lost. When we are faced with too many choices, when everything seems possible, often we can choose nothing. Although we pride ourselves on being intelligent, sophisticated, and free from restrictions, more and more of us suffer from depression, anxiety, sleeplessness, and un-fulfilling relationships. We turn to drugs, medication, and all kinds of therapies, but our conditions linger on or return.

In place of reliance on discipline and structure, today there is a great deal of compulsive behavior and addiction, including substance abuse, addiction to technology (TV, Internet, cell phones), workaholism, and addictive patterns in relationships. These unwanted habits, which cannot easily be broken, replace the true discipline and structure that is an integral part of all spiritual practice.

Both Zen and Judaism are based on strong discipline. In Zen practice and in the observance of mitzvot, you are called on to stop certain activities and patterns of thought, whether or not you want to, or see any value in doing so. In addition, you are also called on to adopt new behaviors that may be uncomfortable at first. However, the restriction of movement, actions, and choices that these practices require actually assists by harnessing your energy and focusing your life. You are taking charge of random impulses and desires, which scatter your forces and lead nowhere. As new ways of being become established, you grow strong. This ultimately brings power and freedom to your life.

## Stopping the Churning Self

Both mitzvot and the practice of mindfulness require you to stop living on automatic and become aware. In fact, stopping is the first point you learn in Zen practice. When you come into the zendo, you stop talking, running here and there, and looking around. You quietly take off your shoes, place them in the shoe rack, put your coat in the closet, and leave whatever baggage you've brought with you at the door.

Usually a student is present as a doorman, so you do not enter unattended. You do not necessarily talk to this person, smile, or greet him in the usual way. Instead, you simply come as you are. Nothing is demanded of you, so you can leave your social persona behind. You do not have to smile if you are sad or engage in frivolous conversation if you feel like being still. You are not coming to the zendo to seek your sense of self from others or become whatever they want of you. Instead, you simply bow to the person, acknowledging and thanking him for his presence and effort.

Then you go to the entrance of the meditation hall and stop again. You place your hands in gassho (palms together), stand there, and feel the floor under your feet, the air on your face, become aware of where you are. Most of the time, we race from one activity to another, one relationship to the next. Now, as we stop, we become fully aware that past activities are over; we are in a completely new moment in time. We become aware of *this* moment, *this* step, *this* breath. This stopping is vital and crucial. It is the beginning of mindfulness.

If we look honestly at our lives, it is easy to see how difficult it is to stop ingrained behaviors and responses. It is so natural to be at the mercy of automatic, repetitive, often unconscious responses. We seldom see the person or situation we are facing. Instead, we are run by old patterns, repetitive thoughts, persistent desires, fierce appetites, and exhausting obsessions, trying to find solace from them in our actions and relationships.

In fact, it could be said that few of us are here at all. We're just playing out a preset scenario with others as supporting actors, everything revolving around our particular wishes and dreams. Again, this is the opposite of mindfulness. This is a life of self-centered obsession and absorption, which can only bring conflict and despair. Another name for it is samsara, the cycle of birth and death.

One-pointed mindfulness, which brings us into the present moment, is a powerful medicine for this disorder. What is this mindfulness exactly? What does it take to really pay attention to a person, a tree, a step we take? What gets in the way? Ultimately, all of Zen practice revolves around developing this precious capacity and applying it in our lives.

## Attention! Attention!

A monk asked a Zen Master, "Teach me the essence of Zen."

The Zen Master answered, "Attention."

"What else?" asked the hungry monk.

The Zen Master replied, "Attention, attention."

"There has to be something more," the disconcerted monk demanded.

"Attention, attention, attention," said the teacher.

Everyone looks for something complicated and elaborate in order to solve the problems of life. But this Zen Master had a different prescription, one that was simple, clear, and abundantly available. Just pay attention. Be awake, be aware.

Paying attention wakes you up from the fog, fantasies, slumber you usually live in. In mindfulness practice, you place your precious attention fully on the present moment, whatever it may be right now. You pull your attention away from hopes and longing, plans, memories, and persistent dreams. In order to do this it is necessary to stop trying to change, fight with, control, judge, or use the world you live in. Instead, you greet whatever comes with attention, acknowledging it as it is right now. This unvarnished attention contains no interpretations or manipulations. You simply become present to the world before you, to the incredible gift and wonder before your eyes.

Your attention is your life force. What you attend to increases; your attention feeds it energy. What you withdraw your attention from inevitably fades. Children often do everything possible including many negative behaviors, to get the attention they so hungrily seek. Attention is equated with love. When someone pays real attention, we feel as though we are loved. When attention is withdrawn, we may feel insignificant or rejected. It's easy to develop an addiction to receiving attention from others in order to sustain our sense of self. In Zen practice we turn this around. Rather than seeking attention we give it, not only to the world around but to ourselves. The practice of mindfulness, or of attending, can therefore also be called the practice of giving and receiving love.

## The Practice of Mindfulness

In mindfulness practice when you cook, you pay total attention to each vegetable you chop for the soup. When you sweep, your full attention goes to the broom, the floor, and the sweeping. You direct your attention to where you are standing, what you are doing, feeling, thinking, and also to whoever may appear in front of your eyes. When you love, you love completely.

You pay attention in a unique manner. You do not ask for things to behave in a way that suits you or fulfills some fantasy you may have. There are no hidden expectations or demands. You just fully attend to, and thus value, whatever appears. When you are able to do this, you will not perceive a problem with anything. And as that happens, everything will fall into perfect place. This kind of attention is like sunshine that warms whatever it may touch. As you attend in this manner, you also bring yourself out of hiding, becoming present and available. Automatic behaviors, obsessions, and compulsions have less and less chance to invade your life.

## The Practice of Mitzvot

The Jewish form of mindfulness practice is the observance of mitzvot. They also constitute a way of stopping impulsive, random behavior and attending carefully to where you are, what the time is, what's going on, and what mitzvah is required of you. Mitzvot create a structure of mindfulness for your life.

Most understand mitzvot to be good deeds. This is not necessarily so. If an individual does what seems like a good deed whenever it may strike him to do it, it's not a mitzvah. It's a good deed, which is wonderful but something else. The Lubavitch Rebbe said, "Doing good is not about being nice. You can do nice things all day long for many people, but it could be all just more service of your own self, food for your own ego. God made a world where people would need each other, not so you could be nice but to give you the opportunity to escape the confines of your own self." Mitzvot not only dissolve the negative ego, but they are also food for the soul. Specifically speaking, there are positive and negative mitzvot, actions you are instructed to take and actions you are to refrain from. All mitzvot are derived from Torah and include many specifics surrounding them. There are special times and circumstances in which to do mitzvot and times to refrain. Each mitzvah, when done in the prescribed manner, affects all aspects of your life and the lives of others.

There are a total of 613 mitzvot, though they do not all apply at the present time. Certain mitzvot are only for women, others only for men. Women are exempt from some mitzvot that have to be performed at a specific time, due to their responsibilities caring for children. Their mitzvot revolve around their duties, their life cycle, and the nature of their souls. Some mitzvot are related to the land and can only be done in Israel. Others could only be done when the Temple stood and certain ceremonies took place there. Some are easy to understand, others puzzling. Some are called decrees (*chukkim*), and even though they do not seem to make sense, are to be followed as given. These mitzvot were derived by the sages of the Great Assembly, and from an Orthodox point of view cannot be altered based on passing circumstances. Other Jewish denominations view them differently. This is a great question in Judaism, with many ramifications and points of view.

Where I grew up, everything I did revolved around the mitzvot. My grandmother Devorah always reminded me that if the Jews do not keep the mitzvot, the world will be filled with danger. Foods, plagues, loneliness, and loveless marriages will all follow. We must always know right from wrong.

"You told me already, Grandma," I would say.

"But you haven't learned yet. And if I don't teach you, then who will?

"I'm listening, Grandma. I'm doing my best to fit in."

"Prove it to me. Repeat the mitzvot you must keep, this minute!"

I didn't want to, but fear came in ripples when I tried to say no. The fear never touched my grandmother, though. How could it? She was stalwart in her love of God, unmovable, a rock among women. There was nothing she couldn't accomplish either. She ran the family business, cleaned the house spotless, and raised eight children, just like that.

"Why should I repeat the mitzvot again? I know God is helping us right now."

"You *know* it?" She was dumbstruck.

Nobody here was allowed to just know anything. If it wasn't written, it wasn't so. Only the sages could *know* it.

"And why exactly should God help us?" she continued, distraught. "Do we deserve it? Do you, do I?"

"If you don't deserve it, who does?" I said, "You do every mitzvah there is and you even start cooking for Shabbos on Thursday. Everyone's invited. Your house is always open for anyone to eat. And God sees it."

"So, now you know what God is seeing? It's pride speaking out of your mouth. Repeat the laws to me this minute. Then follow them."

I had no choice but to start repeating the mitzvot my grandmother taught me, in the fading evening light.

"God has commanded that we must observe and follow his holy ways.

"We belong to God and to God only. Without him we are only dust. It is him we must worship, thank, and bless. We must do his will and his will only. We are forbidden to desecrate Sabbath. We are forbidden to sing unholy songs. A woman must be constantly modest. Lust is forbidden for all. Rather than bow down to an idol, we must be willing to give up our life. God is good and God can be vengeful. Observe and remember. It's a single command."

"All right, so you can say the mitzvot. But can you live them?" Her large hands were clenched beneath her enormous bosom. "I'm worried about you. You can't be weak, I won't allow it, too much is needed from you. All your relatives who died in the war . . . you have to live for all of them now."

"How can I?"

"Someday you'll know," she breathed deeply, "when you learn how to become a real Jew."

Of course I had no idea how I would ever become a real Jew, one like my grandma, who went straight ahead, followed the laws 100 percent, and never looked to the right or the left. My heart wandered and strayed everywhere. I wanted to taste the whole wide world and meet all the people in it.

"Don't worry, I try, Grandma."

She zeroed in, "Tell me once when you really tried. Someday, if God is good to you, you'll have an idea of what it means to really try. And I only hope someday, someone comes and teaches you what it means to really try." Of course neither she nor I, at that moment, had any idea that one day a Japanese samurai Zen Master would be coming to teach me how to really try—how to become a true Jew at last. But in Borough Park, Brooklyn, there was only one way to become a real Jew: study and fill your life with the mitzvot, one day after the next.

## Observing the Mitzvot

Even though I found it daunting, it was also fascinating and surprising to discover what exactly these mitzvot asked of me. It was even more amazing when I started doing them again as an adult. There was no telling what would happen then. Ultimately I discovered that the most important aspect of doing a mitzvah was the relationship that was being established between myself and God, who commanded them. It was as though a line of communication was being established. The Torah states that the highest level of doing a mitzvah is *l'shmo*, just because it has been asked of you, not for any personal benefit but for its own sake.

Mitzvot have many functions and effects. One function is mindfulness: to keep you constantly aware of where you are, what the circumstances are, what time it is, who is in front of you, and which mitzvah is required at this particular moment. You are not to respond to life helter-skelter, but realize that everything is an opportunity to do an appropriate mitzvah. When you take that point of view, even painful situations become a chance to grow. Not only do you uplift or heal the situation, but you also bring light into the world.

Following the mitzvot cuts into obsessive behavior and addictions. For example, if you are a workaholic and you keep the Sabbath, when you see that the time is coming, no matter what you are doing or feeling, you must stop everything so you can prepare. Sabbath requires a complete letting go of all kinds of activities. Even though it may be difficult to stop what you are doing or interrupt an automatic response, each time you do so, you are no longer at the mercy of compulsive feelings but are utilizing your energy in ways that elevate your life.

Needless to say, it is almost impossible to keep all the mitzvot that pertain to you. At times you can keep more, at other times less. Sometimes mitzvot bring great joy, other times conflict or distress. There are times you cannot wait to fulfill a mitzvah, other times when you cannot run away far enough. By going against your natural rhythms or in a different direction from the present culture and fashions, the mitzvot set up a dialectic within, a struggle and dialogue. This struggle itself is good and productive. It causes you to constantly interact with the basic questions of your life. In acknowledging the difficulty of observing mitzvot, the Torah states that different individuals have mitzvot that pertain particularly to them.

## Escape from Slavery

Many have difficulty with the mitzvot because they feel keeping them takes their freedom away. Rather than fulfilling external commands, they want to listen to and live from the spirit within, as in Zen practice. But this fundamental between Judaism and Zen is only on the surface. Before a Zen student becomes able to live fully from the spirit within, there are many years of discipline, structure, practice, many years of breaking helter-skelter responses and automatic habits. The mitzvot do this in one way, Zen practice in another.

Torah constantly states that Jews were brought forth from slavery in Egypt. Metaphorically, Egypt is a place of confinement, difficulty, and slavery to the material world, the body, senses, and their endless demands and complaints. It was also the place of slavery to the Pharaoh, who represents any person or situation that assumes negative dominion and authority over you. When in Egypt, the Jews could not liberate themselves but were freed through divine intervention. This does not refer only to days of old. Even though we may have apparent freedom, how often we feel trapped and enslaved. When times of vulnerability or upset come, when someone is ill or dying, when an important relationship or job is lost, the experience of helplessness and enslavement often arises. Freedom to live and act fully may be taken away, and we lose a sense of being in control.

In order for slavery to end today, according to Torah, divine intervention must still take place. But divine intervention is only the beginning. As in Egypt, true freedom from slavery was ultimately accomplished through each individual's acceptance of the mitzvot. These very same mitzvot are still the means of divine intervention available today.

When mitzvot are made the authority in your life, they come before the demands and dictates of everything else. This takes power away from all the false authorities trying to control you. Look at the authorities in your life today, to who or what you give power. When you follow the mitzvot, you do not listen to the voices and demands of the outside world or of false authorities. As the mitzvot become your authority, your enslavement to others (and to yourself) diminishes, and you become able to enter the promised land within. What once might have seemed to restrict you, now becomes your pathway to freedom.

This practice is available to non-Jews as well. There are seven Noahide laws in Torah, which are specifically intended for non-Jews (explained in Chapter 8). Any non-Jew who wishes to join the Jewish people is not only welcome to do so, but is to be greatly welcomed and honored. The Torah says that not even the highest sage can stand in the place of a convert. (This is discussed more fully below.)

## The Zen Path to Freedom:
## Going to the Other Shore

Zen students also seek freedom; they call this going to the other shore. They seek to escape samsara, the cycle of birth and death, desire, craving, satiation, and then more desire. They also seek freedom from false authorities and delusions within.

Samsara, life as usual, can certainly become a form of slavery. In samara you find the pain of alternation or change. You are subject to birth, old age, and death, hot and cold, love and hate. You continually experience gain and loss, good and bad, hope and disappointment. You are tied to the material world, to your body, senses, hopes, desires, and fears that drive your life. All of this keeps you revolving on the wheel of karma, unable to break free. So, where is this other shore? How do you find it? By sitting in endless meditation, blocking out the world? Is this the equivalent of a Zen mitzvah? No, not at all.

The way to escape bondage in Zen practice is different. I got a taste of it at my first group interview with my Zen Master about six months after I became a preparatory student.

In those days new students were called preparatory students. There was a group of us going to sesshin (retreat) for the first time and none of us had yet had an interview with the Zen Master. This interview was being held during winter retreat, when it was extremely cold. The zendo had no heat, and the doors leading to the Japanese garden in the back were wide open. Preparatory students were seated in the back, near the open door. Icy winds blew in over us to encourage stronger sitting and deeper concentration. It worked the opposite way for me. I piled on three sweaters and was shivering and angry, unable to concentrate on anything but the cold.

Suddenly a monk came to the back and told the new students it was time for us to see the master. Everyone rose and walked single file upstairs to the interview room. Totally freezing and unwilling to go anywhere, I sat right where I was. A few minutes later, the same monk flew back in, yanked me off the cushion, and pulled me upstairs. Horrified, I had no choice but to follow.

When I entered the dokusan room, it was dark. The Zen Master was grandly seated in his black robes in front of a single candle that was burning. The students were sitting in a row, terrified, in front of him. The flames from the candle flickered wildly. No one moved. Dead silence.

Finally he said, "Any questions or comments?"

The silence deepened.

Suddenly I called out, "It's freezing down there."

"Then freeze!" he growled fiercely and rang his bell to indicate the interview was over.

Although we did not know it at the time, he taught us how to escape the pain of freezing. When you are cold, freeze. When you are hot, burn. When you are sad, grieve. Whatever comes, welcome it 100 percent, nothing left over. *Leave no traces.* Do not escape your experience. Do not avoid it in any way. This is mindfulness taken to its fullest extent. Welcome whatever comes to you, with no reservations. The bondage of life is caused by struggle against and resistance to whatever is going on. It is the endless desire for things to be different that causes entrapment. When the struggle against life disappears, when you embrace each experience completely, where is your slavery then? At that point, samsara turns to nirvana, a place of oneness and joy.

## Channeling Divine Energy

Why isn't it enough to live our lives 100 percent as life comes to us?

What is the need for something extra? Why take on the mitzvot? Jewish practice says that the mitzvot go beyond the natural world as we know it. They are channels for drawing divine energy into the world,, forms through which this energy manifests itself. When you take on these mitzvot you are healing the entire world, uniting matter and spirit. Each mitzvah has enormous reverberations, although we are unaware of them. Mitzvot bring illumination and uplift many beings, seen and unseen. They not only guide and protect us, but protect the whole universe.

That is why the mitzvot need to be done precisely, why it's important to understand the fine points. If they are not done precisely, the effect is not there. This is similar to karate, where students are taught to make specific moves. These moves not only bring forth certain energies but also protect the student from receiving blows. The same is true for the mitzvot.

At this point, you may wonder what these mitzvot actually are. Although a full exploration of the mitzvot is beyond the scope of this work, some basic ones are described below. Some of these mitzvot relate to your relationship with God; others are between man and man. There are mitzvot that relate to ways of serving God, specific rituals, festivals, and times of celebration. Other mitzvot are mentioned in chapters that examine different life cycles and issues.

Some of these mitzvot seem confusing, others impossible. Learning the specifics of mitzvot may make it more doable. Other mitzvot become clarified as you take them on. One mitzvah tells you to love God with your whole heart. You may begin by not knowing who or where God is or how to love him, or anyone. That's perfectly fine. As you practice the mitzvot, you will begin to understand, to have your own experience. Be patient and remember the Torah's instructions, "Do and you will see." If you are interested in exploring the details of the mitzvot further, they are elaborated in the volumes of the Shulchan Haruch.

## Taking the Zen Precepts (Jukai)

There are no divine commandments in Zen practice, no preset beliefs to adopt. There is just practice, practice, and more practice. Due to the fact that change is constant, Zen does not set up rules and regulations that apply under all conditions. Instead, you are to become fully present to the moment, to the flow of life as it presents itself. As each moment is entirely new, there can be no preset response. The thrust of Zen is to free you from external injunctions and restrictions, to allow action to arise in a natural and spontaneous way. When action arises from an enlightened state of mind, it can be trusted and will be perfectly suited to the situation at hand. Your own practice always leads the way.

And yet many Zen students take the precepts. They are similar to the mitzvot in important ways, but different too. They are considered guidelines of practice, a kind of vow you take that directs your behavior. The precepts are said to be the manifestation of wisdom and ways of living in harmony with that which is best for all. Keeping the precepts helps dissolve attachments and delusions. Choosing to take the precepts (receive Jukai) can be a turning point in practice, a public declaration of dedication. It can also signify formally becoming a Buddhist.

Dogen Zenji, a thirteenth-century patriarch of Zen, said that taking the precepts is the heart of Zen; he is referring to making a l vow for your life with deep intention. When you take the precepts, you vow to live a life of mindfulness, practice, and dedication to the good of all. You also vow to relinquish delusion, on which all negative activity is based. The vow and intention are central and guide you through difficult times.

Different precepts are taken, depending on whether you are a lay student or you become ordained as a monk or a nun. More precepts are applicable to monks and nuns, who shave their heads as part of their vow to awaken for the good of all. The basic precepts are listed below.

## Guidelines for Jewish Practice

### ONE MITZVAH A DAY

Take note of the areas in your life where you feel enslaved, areas where you find it difficult to move forward freely. See what actions you normally take. Choose new actions in those areas, based on a mitzvah that is listed below. Replace the old behavior with a mitzvah and see what takes place.

A very important and simple mitzvah is to say the Shema twice each day, in the morning and evening. "Hear O Israel, the Lord our God, the Lord is One." *Shema Yisroel, Adonoi Elohanu, Adonoi Echod.* This prayer takes only a moment, but it is the basic prayer of all the Jewish people, one that is said from childhood on. During all religious services, the moment it is said, it reverberates deeply within and brings you into a different state of mind. It is said that when people were dying in the Nazi camps, this prayer was often on their lips.

There are many mitzvot listed below. See which one speaks to you. Take one on for a day. Learn more about it. Read what you can. Even if it is only a simple action, do it fully, with your whole heart and mind. The next day do another. Spend one week this way. See how this affects you and others. Each mitzvah has a life of its own. Some will especially speak to you, others may not. Don't make this a source of pressure, guilt, or anxiety, but a wonderful adventure. This is a lifelong journey of the soul.

## Foundational Mitzvot

### I AM YOUR GOD

It is a mitzvah to believe there is a God who controls the world and watches over everything that happens. The world is not random; one is not left alone. When you find yourself doubting, wondering, or feeling abandoned, stop and choose this mitzvah. This may be difficult to do; it may feel false to believe something you have no experience of. Start by considering the possibility. Act as if it were true. See what it would be like to actually believe this. What starts as a belief can become a vivid reality. The more you practice this mitzvah, the more you will begin to experience the presence of God in the world.

### LOVE YOUR GOD WITH ALL YOUR HEART, ALL YOUR SOUL, AND ALL YOUR MONEY

This is profound and complex. But how it is possible to love God in such an unconditional manner when there is so much suffering to endure in life? In Judaism, however, love is not simply a feeling. It is based on actions and thoughts. Though you may not have control over your feelings, you can always control your thoughts, deeds, and words. This mitzvah says that all of your thoughts, deeds, and resources should be directed toward God in a positive way, no matter how you feel. This is love in action. Whatever you do, whatever you have, whatever you give or receive, do it in order to honor God. The fruit of this mitzvah becomes real in your life, when you actually begin to feel this love, not only for God but for all creation.

## SERVE GOD
## WITH ALL YOUR HEART

Prayer is the service of the heart. The essence of this mitzvah is to pray every day, first to praise and bless God, then ask for your own needs, and give thanks. One can wonder whether God really needs our praise? That is not the point. The point is that we need to attain a state of mind and heart filled with praise and thankfulness. All of the other mitzvot are a way of serving God as well. Take a moment to stop and dedicate whatever you are doing to the service of God. This puts the activity in an entirely new context.

## DO NOT WORSHIP OTHER GODS;
## DO NOT BOW DOWN TO A STATUE OR AN IDOL
## OR ANY LIKENESS OF A HUMAN

This mitzvah is mentioned constantly throughout Torah and is referred to as *avodah zorah*. It is a warning not to make any images, pictures, or likenesses of God, not to worship anything that has form, or anyone you find in the world. This is a profound way to keep you from over attachment and clinging to this world. All attachment and worship are directed to the infinite invisible—God. This mitzvah also protects you from being controlled by authorities, gurus, and individuals of all kinds. As our hearts are so eager to worship and adore, and as this feeling is displaced so readily, this mitzvah is a ticket to freedom and protection from all kinds of disappointment and pain.

### ADMIT YOUR SINS

It is a mitzvah to admit your sins and errors. Verbally confess your wrongdoings on an ongoing basis, from the bottom of your heart. Along with true regret, you must make a strong resolve not to do the deed again. In this manner, Jewish practice provides a daily means of cleansing yourself, removing guilt and sorrow, and becoming renewed.

## Mitzvot Related to One Another

*Love your neighbor as yourself.* This is the fundamental principle of Torah, and many other mitzvot are derived from it. You are to have mercy on your friends, their money, and their honor, just as you would on yourself. In order to love God fully, you must fully love his creation. Many cannot love themselves, and most are in conflict with neighbors. This is where the practice of Zen becomes vital. As we sit, we become able to love and we discover who out neighbor truly is. For most of us, fulfilling this mitzvah is a lifelong path.

Some other mitzvot connected to this include not committing adultery, not stealing, killing, or infringing on someone else's boundary or rights. Positive mitzvot include visiting the sick, comforting mourners, escorting the dead, helping a bride get married, and making peace.

*Open your hand and give many times.* It is a mitzvah to give charity (*tzeduka*) to the poor. You are more obligated to do this mitzvah than any other. It says that whoever sees a poor person and turns his eyes away, transgresses. You should not think that by giving charity you are losing money; just the opposite, you will be blessed. There are many forms of charity—money, time, attention, work, giving someone else the benefit of the doubt. Give with an open hand and heart, and your life will be fruitful. The highest way of giving is simply to give, wanting nothing in return.

*Love the stranger.* It is a mitzvah to love the stranger. You are not to reject a stranger but show love by giving her food and clothing and welcoming her. You are also to know the spirit of the stranger. This means taking time to find out and honor who she is and not impose your expectations on her. Of course when you know the spirit of a person, she is no longer a stranger but becomes a friend. A stranger here also refers to a convert.

*Escort guests; accompany your guests to the door.* It is a big mitzvah to escort guests; this is said to be greater than anything. Abraham, the forefather of the Jewish people, is the finest example. He fed passersby, gave them something to drink, and escorted them to where they were going. Receiving guests is considered more precious than receiving the holy spirit. And escorting guests is even greater than that. Escort your guests on their journey. Some escort their guests to the door, others to the elevator or down to the street. A few go with them to get transportation and a very few even escort their guest all the way home.

*Honor your father and mother.* It is a mitzvah to honor your mother and father. This means giving them food, drink, and clothes, and supporting them according to your ability. This does not refer only to financial support as they get older, but to the warmth and closeness of your company and regard. This mitzvah may be difficult if there is conflict between your parents and you. The Torah says to do it anyway. The more conflict there is, the greater the obstacles you have to overcome in doing a mitzvah, the greater the mitzvah, the deeper the reward and the more light you bring down into the world. Honor your parents even after their death. By keeping this mitzvah, you return good to the one who did kindness to you.

*Be fruitful and multiply.* It is a mitzvah to marry and have children. By doing this mitzvah, you become a partner with God in creation. You also have an opportunity to teach your children, to love and grow, and to experience what it's like to be a parent. Often you cannot fully forgive or understand your parents until you become a parent yourself. Each stage and role in life is precious in developing all parts of yourself.

*Mourn for your relatives.* No one is to be thrown away or forgotten. You are obligated to mourn for your relatives. As you mourn, search your deeds and the meaning of your life, and then make necessary corrections. The loss of a relative is a time of trial and repentance. Every life is precious and it's passing should not be made light of. Also, it should not be in vain.

*Watch what you say and do what you promise. Do everything that comes out of your mouth.* It is a huge mitzvah to keep your word. The word is built upon honesty and trust. Your word is precious. By keeping your word you strengthen both yourself and the world you live in. There are many mitzvot related to words and speech. By our words we build the world or tear it down.

*Do not gossip or listen to gossip (lushen hora)*. This is one of the biggest mitzvot. You are not to gossip, insult, lie, deceive, or slander. When you listen to gossip, your fellow man is brought down. This can be so serious that when you insult someone in public and he blushes, you are considered to have killed a part of that person's soul.

*Judge one another favorably*. Give everyone the benefit of the doubt. This mitzvah seems to go against our natural inclinations. We often look for what is worst in a person or become suspicious at the drop of a hat. But doing so not only harms you, but the other person as well. It is an important mitzvah to find the best in all. If a negative situation arises between you and someone else, search for the most positive way to explain it. Give everyone the benefit of the doubt.

*Pay your worker on the same day the work is done*. An important but often overlooked mitzvah is to pay someone who has worked for you on the very same day the work was done. When you hold back or delay wages, it is as though you have taken part of someone's soul. You don't know if that person is counting on the wages. You don't know what suffering he will go through if he does not receive his pay on time. It is crucial to be fair and honest in all business dealings. The world is established on truth and fair dealings. When you are scrupulously honest in your business dealings, it is as if you have kept the entire Torah.

*Return a lost object to your brother.* It is a mitzvah to return a lost object. It is said that our belongings contain a portion of ourselves. It is crucial to make sure that each person has the things that belong to him or her. If you see something that has been lost, make sure you return it as quickly as possible. You can even go further with this mitzvah when you take note of anything that may have been lost by another and try to return it, such as self-worth, hope, joy in life, and inspiration.

## Mitzvot Related to the Service of God

*Remember the Sabbath day to make it holy.* The Sabbath is a foundation of Jewish practice. There are many laws pertaining to activities to do and to refrain from doing on the Sabbath. The purpose of these laws is to create a vessel, a structure in which to experience deep peace, stillness, and connection to God. These laws protect you from the endless distractions, demands, and restless activity you are involved in all week long. This is a day of rest, prayer, communion with God and with one another. Over the centuries it has been said that the Jewish people do not keep the Sabbath; it is the Sabbath that keeps them.

*Gather together to observe, honor, and rejoice on the festivals.* Many holidays and festivals punctuate the Jewish calendar. It is an important mitzvah to stop what you are doing and gather together to observe, celebrate, and honor them. This includes prayer, singing, Torah study, dancing, and feasting. The more joy, the greater the mitzvah. Jewish practice celebrates all aspects of life, lifts it up and infuses it with joy.

❧ *Circumcise your s male child on the eighth day after his birth.* It is a mitzvah to circumcise a boy when he is eight days old. This unites him in both body and spirit with God and establishes him as part of the Jewish people. In Jewish practice the physical and spiritual are always intertwined.

## Guidelines to the Practice of Zen

### PRACTICE MINDFULNESS

Decide to practice mindfulness, one day at a time. Choose a place or activity to start. Perhaps you'll be particularly mindful during breakfast and clean up, perhaps when you shower in the morning, or are on the way to work. Dedicate a specific amount of time to paying complete attention.

Be attentive to your body, your thoughts, and whatever else appears during that time. Do not react or respond. Just pay close attention to everything. See how you feel. Do this daily. The length of time you do it may increase by itself. Tension and impulsivity may decrease. You may begin to notice many, many things you had glossed over in the past. By becoming mindful, you are welcoming new experiences into your life. As they practice mindfulness, some feel as though they are awakening to a whole new world.

## Basic Precepts

The basic precepts for lay Zen students are stated simply. Each precept is an instruction and a form of meditation in action. Taken together, they describe the life of a Zen student.

*Be mindful and reverential with all life, do not be violent, do not kill.* Avoid killing or harming any living being. Protect and care for of all living creatures. Do not harm other beings.

*Respect the property of others; do not steal.* Do not take anything that is not given. Live simply and frugally. This precept refers to more than not stealing. It means that we are not to covet things in the material, psychological, or spiritual realms.

*Be conscious and loving in relationships; do not give way to lust.* Avoid sexual irresponsibility. Refrain from improper sexual activity. Do not engage in sexual misconduct. Be conscious and loving in your relationships. Always take care of your partner and his or her honor.

*Honor honesty and truth; do not lie or deceive.* Avoid lying or hurtful speech. Do not indulge in incorrect speech, including gossip, slander, and spreading false rumors. Silence is precious; do not engage in frivolous conversations.

*Exercise proper care of my body and mind; do not be gluttonous or abuse intoxicants.* Avoid alcohol and drugs that diminish clarity. Do not take intoxicating drinks and drugs that lead to carelessness. Do not engage in anything that clouds the mind.

*Do not discuss the faults of others.* Never discuss the faults of others or engage in careless, haphazard talk.

*Do not praise yourself while abusing others.* Do not dwell on how wonderful you are as opposed to others. Do not abuse or oppose others or live a life of duality.

*Do not spare the dharma assets.* Do not be stingy about anything. Give of yourself unstintingly.

*Do not indulge in anger.* Do not indulge in negative emotions. Do not contrive fantasies and distort reality, producing negativity of all kinds.

*Do not defame the Three Treasures.* The Three Treasures are the Buddha, the dharma, and the sangha (Buddha, the Absolute; dharma, the teachings, the essential truth; sangha, the community of students). Do not speak against the Three Treasures or harm them in any way.

## Stepping-Stones on the Zen Way (From Both Zen and Tibetan Buddhist Lojong Teachings)

Breathe each breath fully.
Taste it. Enjoy.

When you are hungry, eat.
When you are tired, sleep.

Welcome all of life, no matter what appears.

*Jewish Dharma*

Don't lean on others.
Don't lean on anything.

When someone comes, welcome him.
When he leaves, do not pursue.

Keep your back straight at all times.
It connects heaven and earth.

Value silence. Only speak when it is real.

Pay attention to each step.
It won't come again.

Give up poisonous food whenever it comes to you.

Don't place a head on your own head.
What's wrong with yours, anyway?

Never give up on a person. Never give up on yourself.

Loneliness is unwillingness to communicate freely
with all of creation. Remedy this.

In the heat of battle, silence is best.

Take your full time to drink your cup of tea.

Do not puff yourself up and put others down.
We are all treading the same earth.

*Disciplining Yourself*

We cannot stop the noise, but we can stop ourselves.
We can accept the noise.

What you are at this moment contains
the whole message of what you were.

Place after place is the right place.

CHAPTER 4

# Calming the Restless Mind: Sabbath and Nondoing

*The Sabbath teaches all beings Whom to praise.*
—ABRAHAM HESCHEL

DAILY LIFE CAN BE relentless, filled with constant demands from which there seems to be no respite. Even when we try to rest or spend quality time with friends and family, actually doing so can be difficult. The world calls us away; feelings of pressure, guilt, and obligation arise. Even in quiet moments it is easy to start thinking about our problems or all there is left to do. It is very difficult to stop and truly rest. The need to get off the wheel and stop our compulsive behavior is addressed deeply in both Jewish and Zen practice. In Zen practice, we stop on a daily basis. During zazen we sit still, stop indulging in automatic reactions, and learn to let go of the endless distractions that accost us on a daily basis. Unless we find the time to do so, it is difficult to live a truly human life. Jewish practice also insists that we stop our usual activities, let go of our preoccupation with the external world, learn to deeply rest, and connect to that which truly replenishes us. In order to do so, we are given the practice of Sabbath. The practice of zazen helps us rest on the Sabbath, and the Sabbath gives another dimension to our understanding of what it means to rest.

Sabbath is a cornerstone of Jewish practice. Jews are directed to stop and rest every week on the Sabbath. This is a time to stop usual activities and devote the day to God, family, friends, community, and yourself. On this day you give up distractions, including work, radio, TV, business, money, cooking, travel. It is a time to rest, renew yourself, become settled, and focus on that which really counts. It is also a day of prayer, study, meditation, and connecting with others. By stopping your usual activities you are being forced to spend face-to-face time each week with your family and yourself. In the book of Genesis it is said that God created the world for six days and then stopped on the seventh day and rested. By stopping and resting on the Sabbath you learn to trust God, honor the connection between you, and discover your real role in this world. This concept of resting is profound. It is not only ceasing activity but finding deep replenishment, balance, and surrender. Not only are you renewed mentally, physically, socially, and spiritually, but your compulsive, automatic activities decrease. The Torah states that the rest and renewal available on the Sabbath provide strength and blessings for the coming week. Torah also tells us that it is not the Jews who keep the Sabbath, but the Sabbath that keeps the Jews. Without stopping, resting, praying, and acknowledging who we are and what we are here for, the Jewish people would have been dispersed long ago.

Sabbath itself teaches us how to stop. By taking our hands off the material world, we learn to deeply let go. As we do this, we then realize Who is in charge of our life, where to turn in time of trouble. Torah teaches that on the Sabbath we receive "an additional soul," extra power to make deeper contact with God and with the meaning of our life.

The practice of Zen enhances the Sabbath in many ways. Zazen helps still the restless mind, develop focus, and become truly present for the different moments, encounters, and teachings that the Sabbath brings our way. In our Zen center, we combine zazen and Sabbath observance. During Sabbath afternoon, we do zazen, study Torah, make blessings on the wine (kiddush), offer prayers, and, after the sitting, enjoy including delicious soups and special, traditional foods such as tzimmes and kugel.

## The Jewish Practice of Sabbath

No matter which denomination you belong to, Sabbath is a day of holiness (kedusha) for all. It creates a space and time that transcend the material world and its usual concerns. The Sabbath is a time of homecoming. As Sabbath takes place on a weekly basis, it becomes impossible to stray too far, either from your external or internal home. Everyone comes home for Sabbath and stays together for twenty-four hours. This can be both comforting and unsettling. We all wish to leave home and find our own way. For six days in the week you can do this, but then on the seventh day you are called home. Without the constant returning, you could easily forget who you are, what you are here for, who it is you need, and who it is who needs you. It becomes easy to drift unanchored in an unruly world.

Depending on their denomination, Jews observe and celebrate the Sabbath in various ways and respond to the laws of
Sabbath differently. I've based my description here on the Orthodox and Hasidic way because this was my original experience of Sabbath for many years. I personally saw and tasted
the depth, power, and healing energy of a Sabbath kept according to the law. Judaism has been present for thousands of
years and the other denominations of Judaism—Conservative,
Reform, and Reconstructionist—are relatively new, some aris-
ing only a couple of centuries ago. The various denominations
are all based on, or are reactions to, the Orthodox (Hasidic)
way. Some denominations accept more, others less of the laws,
and all have different interpretations. Before we change or
react to something, it is necessary to know what it is we are
changing or reacting to. Some of the interpretations of the other
denominations are beautiful and life-giving. My choice does
not imply a criticism of them; I understand the impulse and
need to be creative. However, it can also be a slippery slope to
do this with the halachas, the laws of Torah. The entire Torah
is an interwoven tapestry. When you begin pulling out one
thread, it creates all kinds of ripples, loosens others and the
integrity of the whole fabric is compromised, with consequences
that are unforeseen. Once this process starts, there is no end to
it, and the Torah may be altered in a way that could make it
unrecognizable, losing the basic integrity of the revelation
that has kept Torah alive and viable throughout the centuries.

Therefore, even though I cannot usually practice all the halachas, even though I may question some of them, I have a
deep reverence for authentic practice and for the revelation
that brought Torah into the world. I don't want to see it

squandered or adulterated. Some denominations arose out of a desire to let go of many aspects of Judaism and assimilate into the lifestyle and thought of modern times. Torah strongly warns against this, clearly saying that the teachings are eternal and are to be kept throughout the centuries, despite passing fads and cultural changes. One can accept or reject the Torah, one can struggle with it endlessly, but why dilute the truth of what it actually is?

## Preparing for the Sabbath

Without preparation, the Sabbath cannot take place. To begin, before the Sabbath arrives, the home is sparklingly cleaned and food is prepared; the challahs are baked or bought, no cooking or work takes place on the Sabbath, and no fires are lit, in the home or elsewhere. All work stops. You do not travel or interfere with the natural course of the physical world. This is not a day to follow your own desires.

All wear their finest clothing to honor the Sabbath. The time of preparation is filled with excitement and hurry. There is so much to do before the moment comes to set the table, light the candles, make the prayers that welcome the Sabbath in. Beautiful songs are sung in the synagogue welcoming the Sabbath as one would welcome a bride or a queen. In one way, the entire day is a retreat, a time when one is called on to stop, praise God, offer blessings, and remember Who it is that runs the universe. The Sabbath is also a day to receive the fruits of one's labors. One has worked all week long, but this is the day to stop and enjoy delicious food, company, song, and pleasure. Many gifts are available on the Sabbath, and one now has the time to receive and appreciate them.

Where I grew up, the preparation for Sabbath could take a couple of days. There was no greater blessing than to prepare food for the Sabbath. When it was time to start cooking, I could usually be found downstairs in my grandmother's kitchen, working by her side, peeling potatoes, chopping carrots, slicing onions, one by one.

My grandmother would move around the kitchen, checking the vegetables, taking out pots, preparing the dough. Her routine was firm and immovable. She would open and close the oven's large doors. I would knead the dough into challah on her long wooden table. Then we would start peeling carrots for tzimmes, a pudding of carrots, raisins, and prunes. We worked together in the kitchen for hours without saying a word.

"Honor to the King, honor to the King," my grandmother would sing from time to time. God was the King and the Sabbath, his bride. A huge celebration was being made ready. She kept singing this over and over. "If even one person goes away from the Sabbath table hungry," she would declare, "we haven't given real honor to the King."

So we would cook and cook until everything was ready. I would listen to her sayings and songs, but what I felt made no difference at all. I couldn't say a word. We would work in the kitchen that way for hours without ever talking to each other. When I'd stop for a few minutes and look out the window at the few bluebells along the alley struggling to bloom, she'd stomp her foot on the floor. "What are you thinking about? Running to shul to be with your grandpa?" I couldn't say yes, that's where I want to be. "Just keep cooking," she demanded. "Your place is here in the kitchen with me. Chop more carrots, slice more onions; time is going fast." So we chopped and cooked and soon the whole world was filled with the smells of my grandmother's cooking. When I ate her food, though, it made me feel lonely. It made such a difference whose food you ate and who you ate with on the Sabbath. Sabbath food was an offering to God. Each bite you ate could make you strong, or it could act on you in other ways.

"With every bite of food you eat on Sabbath," Reb Bershky said, "God draws you closer into his arms. And you draw God closer too. The food we eat on Sabbath gives us strength and pleasure for the whole week long."

So, when the Sabbath arrived, I would often run down the block to Reb Bershky's table. He knew I was coming and didn't begin until I arrived. As soon as I slipped in the back door and took my seat, he'd picked up his glass of wine, stand at the head of the table, and say the prayers for the kiddush, the Sanctification.

Everyone sat in total silence. Reb Bershky went on a little longer, and then all lifted their wine glasses together and drank. They blessed God and each other. After that he made blessings over the challah and gave a piece to everyone. While the rest of the food was being passed around, all would begin to sing timeless, beautiful Sabbath songs. They were love songs to God, thanking him for everything. From the mouth of each person, including tiny children, the ancient, sweet songs and blessings arose. Those melodies were beautiful and made me strong. They gave direction and held me firmly in their arms.

While everyone was singing, Reb Bershky's wife Miriam passed the chullente, a thick stew with meat, beans, potatoes, and eggs, down the table on a huge silver platter, and everyone took some. At the very same moment, in every house on the block; all the families were eating together.

## Coming to Rest
## and Joy on the Sabbath

Jewish practice teaches that our inability to rest—the cause of our insatiable hunger, restlessness, suffering, and greed—is a lack of connection to God. When you are not in touch with God, do not feel deeply bonded to him, you naturally feel separated and alone. Then you do not know who you are, what you should do, or where you fit in. You might even feel as though the world is resting on your shoulders and not be able to relinquish control. Sabbath observance is the antidote to that.

The Sabbath is the consummate experience of letting go. During Sabbath you know exactly what to do and what to refrain from doing. You do what is given to you to do and leave the rest to God. This is a day of training to know your place in the world and relinquish control. This can seem frightening, as though all could go haywire then. Actually, the opposite is true. When you learn your role, what you are here to do and not to do, letting go of control becomes easy and even natural. You can then return to your place and settle in it. Ultimately, in order to feel true connection and peace, you must know who you are, where you belong, and how to let go of control.

Nondoing is also at the heart of Zen practice. The term "nondoing," or doing nothing, has been deeply misunderstood. It can be thought to mean passivity or not caring. It can seem to indicate laziness or unwillingness to confront what is at hand. Once again, the opposite is true. The *Tao Te Ching* states it beautifully: "The world is ruled by letting things take their course. It cannot be ruled by interfering." Like Sabbath observance, which requires preparation and structure to arrive at a place of peace, nondoing is one of the most active concepts in Zen practice. It urges us to "Do, nothing." This also requires effort, strength, and discipline. Nondoing is the activity of stopping the restless heart and mind. Like the Sabbath, nondoing heals the compulsive, repetitive, negative behavior that so many are in the grip of. Jewish practice focuses on our connection to God in order to quiet the restless heart. Zen practice focuses on the part of ourselves that keeps us agitated. In Zen the compulsive part of us is described as the hungry ghost. The hungry ghost robs us of contentment, taking away our peace and comfort. It is also the part of ourselves that makes it difficult for us to settle down and be at ease.

## Who Is the Hungry Ghost?

A hungry ghost is the part of a person that is driven by greed, anger, and delusion, always seeking approval and gain. When the hungry ghost goes to a banquet, it eats everything offered but does not digest the food or receive pleasure from it. No matter how much it devours, the hungry ghost is left just as hungry as before. Zen practice says that the hungry ghost is a product of karma—an accumulation of our own thoughts, deeds, and actions. It is grasping, restless, and cannot be satisfied, no matter what it receives.

The hungry ghost is not only hungry for food—it cannot be fulfilled or satisfied by any of life's offerings. Its greed, anger, and delusion prevent it from fully tasting and digesting its experience, from absorbing the nourishment and discarding the waste. It refuses to feel loved or fulfilled, to settle down, or to be grateful. No matter how much you give the hungry ghost, it keeps wanting more.

The practice of nondoing and of resting on Sabbath deflates the hungry ghost, takes the steam out of its endless grasping and drives. Nondoing is based on the principle that the more we feed the hungry ghost within, the more we give in to its endless cravings, the hungrier and more desperate it becomes. By simply noticing whatever desire arises and not responding to it, we stop feeding the desire energy. We do not suppress anything but welcome it and watch it arise and then pass away. Neither do we judge, hate, or reject our desires. If we do, we're in trouble. That which we fight, we strengthen. Instead, we simply notice these relentless needs and desires and simply let them go. The process of noticing and not responding, nondoing, is very powerful. Eyes open, wide awake, do not get swept away by garbage.

## Practicing the Laws of Sabbath

Observing the laws of Sabbath also stops the hungry ghost in its tracks. There are many laws regarding the observance and protection of the Sabbath. These laws (halachas) create a structure that permits the Sabbath experience to take place.

Some laws of Sabbath are negative, describing what you are to refrain from doing on this day, others are positive, describing what you are to do. Some of the prohibitions include not working, cooking, lighting a fire, traveling, writing, painting (engaging in creative activity), speaking on the phone, using electronic equipment (no TV, radio, cell phones, etc.). You simply stop interfering with the natural world in any way at all. The world belongs to God and on the Sabbath you give it back to him. Everyone gets to rest, including your guests, workers, animals, plants, and even the earth.

Some of the positive laws include preparing for the Sabbath, cleaning the house until it sparkles, using your finest dishes, getting ready for the celebration. Cooking for the Sabbath meals is done the day before Sabbath begins. The women prepare challah and other wonderful Sabbath foods. It is considered a great mitzvah to have guests for the Sabbath. Some even say that unless you have a guest for the Sabbath, your table and observance are not complete. Although the Sabbath may seem like a day of retreat, it is just the opposite. Everyone joins together; no one is allowed to be left alone.

Sabbath teaches that part and parcel of uniting with God is uniting with one another. Without joining together in community, without offering and receiving nourishment and hospitality, without blessing each person you come in contact with, the spirit of the Sabbath is not present. And ideally this hospitality and generosity is then continued all week long.

Once the Sabbath comes, it is greeted as a queen and is honored in every way. You dress beautifully, kiddush prayers are said, beautiful blessings said over wine and bread. You eat three delicious Sabbath meals and sing love songs for the Sabbath after the meals, praising and thanking God for everything. It is important to study Torah on the Sabbath. There are talks on Torah at synagogue and classes are offered. During the day everyone goes to the synagogue for prayer, Torah reading, study, singing, meals. If someone has been born, you hear about it; if someone has died, you also find out. If anyone is in need, you offer help or consolation. No one is allowed to mourn on the Sabbath. This is a day of joy, celebration, and feasting where you acknowledge and share the gift of life that has been bestowed on you. During the day you give thanks continually for everything, both the bitter and the sweet.

It is a big mitzvah to make love to your spouse on the Sabbath. In fact, a husband is commanded to give his wife pleasure on the Sabbath. The more everyone feels pleasure, joy, connection, the more they experience the divine. This lovemaking not only increases the joy you experience on the day, but is an offering to God and a way of uniting with Him in love and oneness. The Sabbath can be seen as a great aphrodisiac, creating the perfect mood for deep bonding, passion, and love, with candles shining and love songs being sung. The Kabbalah teaches that when a husband and wife make love on the Sabbath, the spirit of God comes to join them and all the world becomes as one.

It is not only love between a husband and wife that is important, but love and forgiveness for one another as well. Whatever happened during the week, the prayers, study, and singing of the Sabbath wash it all away. Reb Bershky taught that it is the Sabbath itself which brings forgiveness. Without the Sabbath no one could find the power to forgive.

The more these laws are followed, the more intensity and energy are available, and the more spiritual rather than social the Sabbath experience can become.

Although some of the Sabbath laws can be difficult to observe, they provide a structure to restore yourself in. Even though you may not be able to follow all the laws, that does not mean you cannot do some. There is a great danger of feeling either inadequate or overwhelmed. The laws do not exist for you to punish yourself with. Do what you can. Focus on what you have done, not what you cannot do. Some feel if they can't do it all, there's no reason to do anything. They measure themselves against a standard that may be impossible to meet. Others fear doing even a little, feeling that before they know it, they'll get pulled into doing all. Both are traps. Sometimes keeping the Sabbath is easy; you cannot wait. Other times, it feels impossible; all you want to do is escape. Both feelings are natural and perhaps inevitable. But whatever you do, even a little step makes a big difference in bringing the blessings and peace of Sabbath into the world. It is very important to realize that the true spirit of Torah is always one of celebration and love. Sabbath is a time to have joy and pleasure; it is a respite from suffering of all kinds.

## Sabbath and Mindfulness Practice

In one sense, Sabbath is another form of mindfulness practice. Distractions are removed on the Sabbath so that we can take charge of our attention and become more keenly aware of God, one another, and ourselves. Zen practice also cultivates mindfulness practice, helping us to become completely present to each moment, each person and activity. As we do zazen all week, mindfulness develops. During mindfulness practice, whatever activity we are engaged in, we do with full attention; we do not run helter-skelter or chase after this or that desire. If we have an itch, we do not scratch it; if we are hungry, we simply experience our hunger and let it be. When it's time to eat, we taste every bite. We do not turn to distractions to soothe, feed, or fill ourselves up. The same is true for the Sabbath, where we keep away from distractions in order to be fully present to the Sabbath experience.

Inevitably, mindfulness practice develops into nondoing—simply being with whatever arises, not judging it, trying to fix it, change it, or impose our ideas on it. Instead, we surrender to the great mystery of life itself and allow it to instruct us. This attitude of noninterference brings true wisdom and healing.

There is a beautiful old Zen story that illustrates the healing power of noninterference and mindfulness. A Zen Master was called to his brother's home. His nephew kept getting into trouble and it seemed nothing could be done. Whatever they tried made matters worse. The nephew was drinking, carousing, sleeping all day, and refusing to go to school. The Zen Master's brother begged him to come and do something to help. Finally the Zen Master agreed to visit for a week.

Everyone was excited and hopeful when the Zen Master arrived, waiting to see how he would handle the wayward boy. When the Zen Master arrived, he unpacked his few belongings and chatted with his nephew casually about this and that. At night when the boy went to the bars, the Zen Master simply went along. Although the boy waited to be reprimanded, the Zen Master did not comment or offer advice. In this manner, he accompanied his nephew all week long wherever he went and whatever he chose to do. On the last day of the Zen Master's visit the boy became uneasy and waited for the scolding he expected. It never came. The Zen Master did nothing out of the ordinary, just spent time with him keeping him company. After they returned home, the Zen Master went into his room to pack. Unnerved, the boy joined him as he prepared to leave. Packed and ready to go, the Zen Master bent down to tie his shoelace, and as he did so, one single tear fell all by itself. The boy saw the tear and was deeply touched and shaken. After the Zen Master left, the boy could not return to his old ways.

The Zen Master did "nothing," and in that nothing everything took place. He did not make a plan to save his nephew; he did not judge, scold, or impose any ideas on him. He did not interfere with the normal course of events in any way. He simply joined the boy, kept him company, experienced his experience. Then at the perfect moment, the perfect response came on its own. It could not have been consciously planned. The action of no action—noninterference—was the greatest action of all. The boy's heart and life returned to where it belonged.

## The Jewish Practice of Returning to Your Place

In Judaism the place is called HaMakom. This is also another name for God. By returning home for Sabbath, by returning to the Torah and to the commandments, you are actually returning to your own place in the world. You are returning to yourself and returning control of the universe back to the One who created it. This does not deny your own personal will. In Judaism the personal will is never negated. It has full run six days of the week, but then on the Sabbath, it is relinquished to the higher will of God. As you do not engage in usual activities, your sense of time alters. Sometimes the day seems to last forever; at other times it passes in one long moment. When you fight and resent the restrictions, time stretches on forever. When you relinquish your personal claims and surrender, you are transported into eternal time, where you find deep fulfillment. The Torah states that your work is fulfilled when it receives the blessing of the seventh day.

As you give up your personal will, as your hungry ghost is forced to stop its restless search, sit still, and be nourished, you discover that only spiritual nourishment can make its cravings subside. All along you have been looking for fulfillment in the wrong places. When you return to your place, take your hands off the world, and practice noninterference, the food you need is readily given and fills you to the brim.

## The Zen Practice of Finding Your Home

Like the practice of Sabbath, zazen also requires that you return to your place; over and over again you take your seat and keep it. Until the bell rings, announcing the end of a sitting, you cannot get up or go away. As you sit still in the silence, little by little, your hungry ghost quiets down and you wake up from the chaos you have been creating. As you sit for a while (either several sittings, an all-day sitting, or even a multiday sesshin, or retreat), your sense of time alters as well. One moment can seem like a thousand years. An hour can pass like a second. You grow to understand that your restlessness and lack of ease may be connected to feeling that there is never enough time to say, understand, or do all that needs to be done. This is because you have not practiced nondoing or let go of control. You are interfering in the course of life. But in both practices, it is easy to see that when you learn the art of nondoing, allow your breath to breathe you, you enter eternal time, where everything is complete.

## Guidelines to Jewish Practice

### PRACTICING THE SABBATH

There are many aspects to Sabbath observance. It is easy to become overwhelmed, so start with one or two things. For example, don't work; take time with your family. Say no to one or two of the endless demands and distractions that come to you all week long. Make the day a time to unwind and rest. Prepare a Sabbath meal to share with others and invite someone over who is lonely that you wouldn't normally include. Spend time being aware of your life and all you have to be thankful for. Offer thanks in any way you feel is suitable.

You may want to find a synagogue or temple where you feel comfortable. Go one step at a time. The best way to begin is to go for services. Some synagogues have "beginner minyans," where the prayers and observances are taught. Here you will also meet others to share your journey with.

Remember the essence of Sabbath, which is nondoing, taking one's hands off the world, letting go of control, recognizing, acknowledging, and honoring a Higher Power, connecting with it in every way.

## Guidelines to Zen Practice

### PRACTICING NONDOING

Zazen meditation is a wonderful basis for the practice of nondoing. Spend some time sitting each day. Watch your thoughts arise but do not chase after them. Return to the moment, return to your breath or to you body sensations. In life, when a strong reaction arises, rather than act on it, stop, breathe, and practice nondoing. Stay in your center and remain aware of what's going on inside. This is active and vital. Remain fully aware without taking action. Let go of judgments and compulsivity of all kinds.

In action, in life itself, try to stop interfering. Let things take their course.

Allow a person to be who they are; allow yourself to be who you are as well.

Stop judging and pushing yourself. Let solutions to problems arise in their own way, at their own time.

Take time to breathe and sense how you are feeling. Give yourself time to just be, sit on a park bench, look at the sky, really enjoy your cup of tea.

There is a wonderful Lojong (Tibetan Buddhist) teaching that says, "Take your whole time to drink your cup of tea."

CHAPTER 5

# Giving Up Defensiveness: Charity and Open Hands

*Let the honor and welfare of your brother,*
*be the same to you as your own.*
—TALMUD

S O MANY OF US live our lives guarded, filled with fear, competition, and defensiveness. We are closed off from our
neighbors, filled with suspicion and prejudice. Our main focus
is to defend ourselves, our possessions, relationships, and territory. The existentialists call this condition *shut-up-ness*, a life
lived in a shell, turned in on itself. When we live in this manner, much of our innate joy, creativity, warmth, and well-being
are obstructed. Ultimately this leads to the paranoia and loneliness so rampant today. Living in this manner we do not realize that we have placed ourselves in a prison and forgotten
where we put the key. The Lubavitch Rebbe says, "We are all
prisoners. But we are sitting on the key."

Both Jewish and Zen practice address this dilemma head-
on. The entire thrust of both these practices is to open the

doors to living fully, to prevent this tragic waste of our lives. Charity and open-heartedness can be expressed in many ways. Many mitzvot in the Torah are dedicated to it, and the entire basis of Zen practice is offering ourselves to life without holding back.

## The Jewish Practice of Welcoming Strangers

One of the most significant mitzvot in Jewish practice, the most important ways of opening our hearts and giving to others, is the practice of hospitality. We are told to welcome strangers and visitors of all kinds. This mitzvah is so important that it is said that in the past the entire nation of Sodom was destroyed because it did not offer hospitality or welcome strangers.

Why is this mitzvah so vital? It is based on the first patriarch, Abraham, who was the ultimate role model for hospitality. It is said that when Abraham was in his nineties, sitting in the heat in his tent and suffering great pain after being circumcised, he saw visitors coming from afar and ran at full speed to welcome them into his tent. The greatness and sensitivity of Abraham's soul led him to see how vitally important it was to open his doors, give to others, make them feel comfortable and cared for, despite the condition he was in. We are further told that although Abraham did not know it, these visitors were angels coming to bless him and also to test him, to see how he would respond to them under dire circumstances.

When you welcome strangers, it is as though you welcome the holy spirit into your life. When you reject those you do not know, understand, or feel close to, you are rejecting a part of God and yourself. As you practice this mitzvah deeply, you learn that there are no strangers, only those you estrange yourself from. The more you estrange yourself from others and create separation, the more constricted you become. Those whose lives are based on defensiveness go against the very heart of this mitzvah. When you refuse to open your heart, life, resources, home, and gifts to others, emptiness and desolation often appear in your life. Although this mitzvah seems simple to do, in truth it is not always so easy.

A few years ago, I moved to a suburb in New Jersey quite close to Manhattan for a couple of years. My children were grown and away that year, I was a newcomer in town, knew no one, and was now living alone. When the Jewish holidays came, on the first day of the holiday, early in the morning, I walked to a new synagogue by myself. Soon after I arrived and sat down, the Rabbi began to speak. He spoke of the crucial mitzvah of welcoming strangers and even said that those who did not welcome strangers could not be considered Jews. I was surprised and delighted to hear this particular talk. It put me at ease about being a newcomer at such an observant place.

After services were over, I went with others into a large room for the kiddush, blessings on the wine, food, and conversation. Many were gathered, wishing each other well, and chatting happily. Although I smiled and tried to greet several people, not one person would meet my eye or wish me a good holiday. I was not welcomed or greeted in any way. Feeling crushed and desolate, I went home feeling much worse than when I arrived.

I thought about this a great deal during the holiday season and decided to try again. About a month later, when the holidays were about to end, on the last day, alone once again, I returned to that synagogue. To my shock, as soon as I arrived, the same Rabbi got up and gave almost exactly the same talk he'd given one month ago, the last time I was there. Once again he fervently urged everyone to welcome strangers, saying how vital the mitzvah was and that they could not be considered Jews if they ignored it. During the rest of the service I thought about how odd it was that I'd heard the same speech twice.

But then, once again, after the services, during the time for food, greetings, and conversation, not one person, including the Rabbi, would look at me or say hello. Something about me just didn't fit in. It's one thing to know what to do, it's another to speak beautifully about what to do, and it's yet another thing to actually do it. A mitzvah that is not put into action is not a mitzvah at all; rather, it turns into the opposite.

That congregation was being tested—how would they actually react to someone new and perhaps different in their eyes? It's one thing to get dressed up for the holiday, feel special, sit and listen to the Rabbi talk about welcoming strangers and agree. It's quite another to be confronted with a real stranger. Each new person who comes into your life is an opportunity to welcome a stranger, to make that mitzvah real and alive.

I could not help but think how completely different this behavior was from the zendo, where each individual, no matter who, is fully welcomed. But even beyond that, in the zendo, no one is ever regarded as a stranger, simply another part of ourselves. Would the Rabbi in that synagogue say that in this respect, those in the zendo were the real Jews?

Unfortunately the experience of feeling unwelcome in synagogues or unable to be part of the community is not only painful, but all too common. After years of struggling unsuccessfully to find the right synagogue, I decided to combine the best of the Zen and Jewish worlds. This has been the impetus for our Jewish zendo. In our zendo, we have only one rule: be kind to one another. Everyone is welcome, as long as they sit quietly in zazen and abide by this rule. There are no trips and games, no judging each other, manipulations, gossiping, or politics. No one is categorized or pigeon-holed as this or that. As we have no hierarchy, no one is up, no one down, no one more or less advanced or more religious than another. Basically, there is nothing to create any power struggles, nothing to gain that someone else doesn't have. We all have life, we all sit and breathe, and when the time comes to stand, we stand up and walk. We listen to the gong when it rings, pray, chant, eat, study, and then go home and live our lives.

## Accompany Your Guests

The entire Torah teaches how to show great sensitivity to the feelings and needs of others, especially those who are in your charge. Therefore the mitzvah of welcoming strangers is elaborated on in depth. It then goes on to say that accompanying guests is even more important than welcoming strangers.

Guests depend on you during the time they are in your care. This is a precious trust. Not only are you to offer your guest your finest food, lodgings, and attention, but when it is time to go, you are required to accompany them as far as possible. Usually this is taken to mean to accompany your guests to the door, make them feel cared for, honored, and special.

However, we can take this mitzvah further. Some accompany guests to their car, down the street, to their bus or train. They make sure the guest is safely on their way. Some very great sages have gone so far as to accompany their guests all the way home. They did not leave them alone for a moment, but constantly looked after their well-being and needs.

## The Zen Practice of Welcoming Those Who Come

A basic dictum of Zen is not turning anyone away. There is a sign at some Zen centers that says, "When he comes we welcome; when he goes we do not pursue." Beyond that, the Zen way of welcoming is sensitive and unique. It gives you the deepest respect possible, allows you to take off your social mask and be who you are. You do not have to smile if you're sad, speak if you feel silent, or pretend to be any way at all. You are not grilled about your background, job, relationships, earnings, beliefs, or marital status—not screened to see if you fit in. You can be just as you are in the moment. Your uniqueness is welcomed.

In fact, the entire practice of Zen encourages you to be true to yourself. No one has to twist himself into a pretzel, invalidate who he is, or live up to the expectations of others to be part of the community (sangha). In fact, this is frowned on. When an individual presents a false persona, the Zen Master laughs and does not respond.

From the Zen point of view, the deepest kindness and generosity is to welcome others exactly as they are. This deep form of welcoming strangers welcomes them in truth and simplicity; it welcomes the authentic person, not the persona or mask that we wear. In many Zen centers, individuals wear plain robes. The purpose of this is so that no one can feel more important if he has fancy clothes or fine jewelry. With robes on it is more difficult to compare oneself to others, or to focus on external presentation. And one, in turn, cannot rely on costumes or props. Who one truly is speaks for itself.

## When He Goes,
## We Do Not Pursue

Another aspect of Zen hospitality is not pursuing someone when it's time for her to go. Zen practice provides a beautiful sense of freedom. When a person leaves, she is not to be pursued. You appreciate the time you had with her but do not impose a sense of obligation or guilt about when she will return. As you learn to give others respect and freedom, you are simultaneously giving it to yourself. It is easy to inadvertently make people feel obligated or guilty. You may want them to stay to keep you happy. It is painful to face separation and you may do anything to keep someone close by. This is not love but possessiveness. It is not the Zen spirit, nor is it an example of truly caring for that person or being kind. Zen practice returns each person to her true nature, to ultimate freedom to follow her heart, do what is needed, stay when she wants, and go when it is time.

Zen deeply recognizes the transience of life, that change is natural and inevitable, and incorporates this in relationships. When others go, you do not pursue. You do not manipulate or inflict guilt, pain, or sorrow. You accompany your guests by sending them forth lovingly, not with a heavy heart. You send them off with an opportunity to return whenever they wish. Maintaining, understanding, and adopting this attitude is a lifelong practice. It is a treasure and a great antidote to sorrow and loss. Chögyam Trungpa, a twentieth-century Tibetan Buddhist Master, describes this condition beautifully when he says that "real generosity is not being possessive."

Beyond this, Zen practice takes us to the place where there is no coming and going, no gain and loss. Ultimately, when someone leaves, you do not feel as though you have lost him so deeply, as the connection remains a part of you, since all are one.

## The Jewish Practice
## of Charity *(Tzeduka)*

In Jewish practice, a fundamental way in which we care for others is through the mitzvah of charity. Charity is a central pillar on which Jewish practice stands. Jews are more obligated to observe this particular mitzvah than any other. The Torah states, "Open your hand. You shall open and give many times. Your brother shall live with you." In answer to the question, Am I my brother's keeper? the Torah says, yes, you are. Often individuals make a big show of giving support to public institutions and ignore those in their own families where relationships are complicated. To eliminate this, the Torah describes the mitzvah of giving charity in great depth. It says clearly, "A poor person who is your relative comes first. If a brother does not give charity to his brother, who else will give charity to him?" Even though it may be easier to give to strangers, your personal feelings do not matter. No matter how you feel about sisters or brothers who are in need, take care of them.

Of course, charity is to give to others as well. The Lubavitch Rebbe describes this mitzvah directly: "The very fact that you know about someone who is in trouble means that in some way you are able to help. Otherwise, why would this knowledge have entered your world?" If a practice is just for yourself, it is not real practice but self-centered preoccupation.

The mitzvah of charity states that you are to give a poor person what he needs. If he has no clothing, clothe him; if he's hungry, give him food; if he's sick, give him medicine. There are many types of hunger and many types of poverty. If a per-

son is lonely, give her company; if she is spiritually impover-
ished, teach her what you know. Give as much as you can af-
ford. Even a poor person who collects charity for himself is
obligated to give. If you see a poor person and turn your eyes
away from him, you have transgressed.

My younger brother, Dovid, has always been one of my
great teachers. Since he was a little boy, he's had difficulty *not*
giving. He cannot bear to see anyone in need. One year, when
he was about sixteen years old, he was a given a new winter
coat for his birthday. It was cold out and we were walking together in the bowery when he saw a homeless person crumpled
asleep in the corner. Immediately he took off his coat and covered the person with it, so he could be warm. There was nothing else he could do. To him, the coat simply came to him, so
he could give it to one in need. He lives his whole life in this
manner. It is who he fundamentally is.

For most of us, it is not like that. Opening and giving is natural for some; for others it is difficult. Whether easy or difficult
does not matter. The Torah says, how you *feel* makes no difference. Just do what must be done, give what is needed. Of
course some gifts are easier to give than others. A good way to
start is by giving what you can.

## Ways of Giving

The ways you give are tremendously important because while
it may seem as though you are giving to others, basically you
are only thinking of yourself. Torah warns that a danger to be
constantly on guard against is giving to enhance your own
ego. When giving, do not it for show. Some give to feel good
about themselves, receive public acclaim, be mentioned in
the right places. This is to be shunned. The best way is to give

anonymously, so that the mitzvah does not strengthen your pride and ego.

In addition, you must always be careful not to embarrass the persons you are giving to or make them feel inferior. In this respect, it is better to give needy persons a way of earning a living than keeping them dependent on you.

Give charity happily. Nothing bad ever comes from it; no one ever becomes poor from giving charity. Those who inspire others to give charity receive more reward than the one who gives.

The highest way to give charity is called *l'shmo*, just giving and expecting nothing back in return. When you give to receive something in return, this is not true giving but simply a form of barter. When you give *l'shmo*, you ask nothing in return, not even that the person be grateful or happy.

Today it can be difficult to distinguish those in real need from those who may be misrepresenting their personal situation. In part as a result, many refuse to give anything, saying, "How can I know if this person is a false or true beggar?" The Hasidic masters answer in this way: "Just give. We are all false beggars in the eyes of God. Those who come to you in need are giving you the opportunity to open your hands and heart, to grow in generosity, to understand the world more fully, and to be deeply grateful for all you have been given and all you have to give.

## The Zen Practice
## of Begging: Takahatsu

A beautiful, ancient part of Zen practice is takahatsu. This is the time when monks put on straw sandals, wear straw hats with large brims, form a line, and go on foot, one behind the other, down into the villages with their begging bowls. The villagers can hear the monks coming from a distance as they chant "Ho, ho, ho" over and over again. When the villagers hear the chanting, they know the monks are coming to receive offerings. The monks never ask directly. They simply stand with their begging bowls, chanting. When a villager comes to make an offering, the monk and villager bow to one another at the same time. Because the monk wears a large straw hat, he cannot see who is making the offering, nor can the person see the monk's face. The giving and receiving are done anonymously. The giver does not become inflated, thinking how wonderful it is that he gives. The one who receives is not shamed, feeling he is needy. The monk is giving the villager the gift of having an opportunity to share. The villager is providing sustenance for the monk who chants, meditates, and cares for him. There is no separation; rather, in this moment the giver and receiver become one. Going a little deeper, we can even ask, What is it that really belongs to us? What is the true gift being given?

About six years ago, I spent a little time at Shogen-ji monastery, doing a sesshin with Yamakawa Roshi. Shogen-ji is an ancient Zen monastery in the mountains of Japan, where things are kept exactly as they have always been. It was a shocking experience that altered my life forever, in both wonderful and difficult ways.

Finally it came time for me to go home. The rainy season had started and it was pouring outside. I was sitting in the back of a car that had come to take me to the airport, my luggage piled beside me. The rain slashed at the windows as I sat waiting to leave. Then suddenly from the corner of my eye, I saw what seemed to be dark shadows pass alongside the car. I quickly turned and looked out the foggy windows and saw some of the monks I had known, lined up, walking barefoot in straw sandals in their robes, one behind the other, down to the village, do takahatsu in the pouring rain. They wore nothing but thin robes and straw hats, and carried empty begging bowls in their hands. Their bare feet, scratched by weeds, walked through pebbles and dirt, unprotected and unclothed. I sat there dry in the car beside my bulging suitcases, suddenly filled with horror at myself and my life. There I was sitting in the car, warm and dry, carrying what at that moment I realized was so much unnecessary baggage.

## The Great Charity of the Sutra Monk

Zen monks go through life with very few possessions. There is an old Zen story about a Zen monk who worked very hard to publish a collection of the sutras, or Zen scriptures. He spent many hours collecting funds to accomplish this. But just as the sutras were about to be published, there was a great flood in the village. People lost their homes and had nothing to eat. The monk took all he had collected and used it to help the villagers.

When things had settled, he went back to collecting once again for the publication. Years passed, and he had again gathered enough funds to publish the precious scriptures. Just then a huge earthquake hit the village. Lives were lost. People were desperate. Once again he used all of the funds to feed, house, and clothe those in need.

By now, years had passed. The monk again resumed collecting funds to publish the sutras. This time he was successful and saw them published. After he died people who saw the sutras said that it was wonderful, but the two other editions he was involved with were far more beautiful.

## The Seven Kinds of
## Generosity Without Money

At Kozen-ji, a Zen temple in Japan, there is a plaque that lists the seven kinds of generosity without money:

- Generosity with eyes—look at someone with gentle eyes.

- Generosity of a harmonious face—smile with a gentle-hearted face.

- Generosity with words—speak kind words.

- Generosity with body—work with sincere attitude.

- Generosity with heart—have deep concern for others.

- Generosity with giving your seat—give your seat to elders.

- Generosity with hospitality—welcome people with a warm heart.

I discovered these wonderful teachings on a calligraphy at the Zen center where I was practicing. For many years they have been my guideposts to Zen in action.

## The Great Treasure of Empty Hands

According to tradition, Dogen, one of the great patriarchs of

Zen who lived in the thirteenth century, made a long journey to China to study Zen. He spent years in the monastery practicing. When he returned to Japan, people happily welcomed him home. Naturally, there was great curiosity about where he had been and what he had learned. When asked what he got in China, Dogen replied, "I came back with nothing but empty hands."

These empty hands are the fruit of Zen practice and the essence of true charity. What are these empty hands? Why are they so deeply valuable?

When your hands are filled with possessions and attachments, are used for grabbing, clinging, and holding on, they become frozen and rigid, unable be generous. Hands like that cannot open easily and give. They cannot touch another, truly feel, comfort, or heal.

Dogen spent years emptying himself of his preconceptions, fantasies, longings, desires, demands. He made himself an empty vessel who could respond to all who called on him, who could open unconditionally, and give. There was nothing left that Dogen was holding on to. He was able to be there for all. He came back with nothing but empty hands. When you are in that condition, you can truly offer whatever is needed of you to anyone who needs it without hesitation.

## Giving the Gift of Yourself

It is important to remember that true generosity or charity involves more than giving money, food, clothing, or shelter. It is not enough to give a few dollars and consider your responsibility met. It is crucial to look a little deeper and see what the person truly needs from you. What is the most potent gift you can give another? An individual you meet may be wealthy, but have deep spiritual, social or emotional hunger. True charity tends to those kinds of needs as well.

About thirty years ago, I met Rabbi Joseph Gelberman, one of the founders of the interfaith movement in this country, who is ninety-six years old and going strong. Rabbi Gelberman personally knew the Jewish religious philosopher Martin Buber and told me the following story about him. When Buber was a scholar in Jerusalem, he sat in his office for hours immersed in prayer and study. One day a student in need came to see him. Martin Buber stopped and spent time with him. The student asked some questions. Martin Buber listened, or so he thought, and replied. The student thanked him for his time and left. Martin Buber felt all had gone well. It wasn't until the next day that Buber discovered that a few hours after he left his office the student committed suicide. The shock of this was so great that Buber closed his books and sat in silence, in deep grief, remorse, and meditation. Over and over he asked himself, what is it that an individual needs when he comes to another person in despair? This question became his natural koan. After living with this question deeply, one day the answer came. When a person is in despair and goes to someone for help, he seeks a presence, through which he will know that, nevertheless, there is meaning. After that, Martin Buber's entire spiritual practice was to truly listen when he listened, not only to listen, but to hear. His only wish was to become completely available and present to whatever and whomever life brought his way. Little by little he became awake to the calls, needs, and cries of all people. His entire life became a form of giving in the highest, most pervasive way.

As you empty yourself of self-centered attachments, you naturally become able to be present, to be generous, and to live with hands and heart that can reach out to everyone. You welcome guests, accompany strangers, and give to all who are in need. Then, depression, defensiveness, and paranoia melt away as real joy and fulfillment enter your life. Some fear that actually practicing this would cause them to be taken advantage of by others, treated poorly in return. However, when you are only thinking of what you can give, not what you are going to receive, when you do not expect anything in return, then it doesn't matter how others respond to you. Your sense of joy and well-being comes simply from the act of giving itself. This is a truly uplifting, life-giving state of mind. Needless to say, it takes practice. This became Buber's life practice, to live and give in this way. He opened to all of life, and in the process of doing so, his joy, strength, and well-being grew.

A beautiful Zen story describes this condition. A Zen Master lived in a simple hut, with few possessions. One night a robber broke in and stole everything the Zen Master had. He was left with nothing. The Zen Master looked through the tiny window of his hut. The moon was shining in. "Ah," thought the Zen Master, "too bad I can't give him this beautiful moon."

## The Jewish Practice of Charity

### OPEN YOUR DOORS

Notice the ways in which you keep your life and doors closed.

Open your doors and invite others over. to others. Have a dinner party, coffee hour, or gathering of any kind. Invite some people to it you might not have previously included. This will open your ability to relate to others, drop your limited conceptions of them, and extend yourself to those in need. To begin, do this with someone you already know, perhaps a relative or neighbor you haven't been close to, then slowly you can extend your outreach.

These are all practices for breaking down inner defensiveness and a quickness to judge, categorize, and reject others. It is based on the idea that we really never see the persons before us, but only our limited images of them. This causes us to lose so many potentially precious and beautiful encounters in life and stay hidden behind an inner wall. When we reach out beyond our range of comfort, life expands and surprising experiences have a chance to take place.

Take special notice of how you treat your guests and remember to accompany them fully in every way.

### LEARN TO LISTEN AND TO HEAR

When someone is speaking to you, stop the dialogue within, focus completely on that person, pay full attention, and really "hear" what she is saying to you.

If she says something that bothers you, don't take it personally. Get out of the way and just be completely available for her. Just think, "How may I serve you?"

If you don't understand fully, stop and ask her to explain.

If appropriate, ask what she needs from you. See if you can give it right away.

### GIVE TO OTHERS

Practice giving every day. Give not only money but something valuable to someone in need.

Spend a little time thinking what it is you truly have to give.

See what you refuse to give others. Make an inventory.

Who needs something of you that you have been withholding? Decide to give it to them today. Give it without demanding anything in return.

Allot a portion of your income to others and give this regularly. Do it anonymously.

## The Zen Practice of Opening Your Hands

### EMPTY YOUR HANDS

What are you holding on to that you need to let go? Let it go today. Empty your drawers; give it away.

Let go of something old and worn out. Let go of a grudge, memory, person, or dream that needs to be freed. See how you feel then.

What are you demanding of others that they cannot fulfill? Let one of those demands go right now.

Who are you holding on to in your life who needs or wants to go? Can you stop clinging so tightly and give that person freedom to be who he is?

Trust that what is for your higher good will come to you naturally.

## Naikan Practice

Naikan is a wonderful exercise (and meditation) developed in Japan. On the surface it is very simple, and yet the with effects are far-reaching and profound. Some have reported being healed of illnesses and emotional upsets by doing this practice deeply and consistently.

Each sitting takes around thirty minutes. Some may take more, others less. When you begin doing this, you can do as little or much as you are moved to. During this time you make three lists. Spend more time on the third list. Do this practice every day.

- *List 1*: Sit down and carefully write out everything you have received today. Be specific. Meditate on the list.

- *List 2*: Write down everything you gave today. Again, be specific; exclude nothing.

- *List 3*: Write down whatever trouble or pain you caused today. Be specific.

This exercise can also be done on a person, or a relationship. When working on a relationship, do three years of the relationship at a single sitting. Start from the beginning of the relationship, asking the same questions: ask, what did I receive from _____?

What did I give to _____? What pain or difficulty did I cause _____?

It is easy to go through life thinking that you are giving all the time and receiving little. Before you know it, you walk around feeling deprived and burdened, resenting that which is asked of you. When you begin to truly do naikan, it is easy to see that the opposite is so. When you stop and really pay attention, you will see how much you are constantly being given and how little you give in return. As you practice naikan, you naturally wish to correct this imbalance, and begin looking for ways to do so. It becomes easy and wonderful to give.

It is also easy to begin to think that you are being harmed or slighted in some way. It is less natural to notice the ways in which you cause trouble or pain for others. The purpose of the third list is not to create guilt but to wake you up, make you aware and sensitive as to how you affect others and how often others go out of their way for you. This again will correct your unbalanced perceptions and make you not only more grateful but more aware of and careful about the ways in which you behave.

Naikan is fantastically powerful when done with sincerity. Naikan retreats are sometimes held in retreat centers. (The Todo Institute in Vermont sponsors these retreats regularly.) During a retreat; participants do naikan for many hours a day. The group facilitator cooks for the participants, brings them food, and intermittently suggests areas to do naikan on. From time to time, the participants reads their lists to the facilitator. The facilitator listens and says nothing in return but, "Thank-you for doing naikan." These retreats are a form of meditation. During them, you have an opportunity to look over your entire life and relationships and get a deep sense of what you have really received, from whom, and what you have given in return. You also have time to become aware of the difficulties you may have caused. Again, this is not for the purpose of creating guilt but for balancing our feelings of having been wronged. A great deal gratitude arises during these retreats as well as some remorse. Many leave the retreats with a sense of deep renewal and an ability to relate to others in a different way. There is often a great desire to give more, as well as a greater sensitivity to the feelings of others. All of us naturally want to be open and giving. Deep within we realize that defensiveness is a form of constriction and illness. Defensiveness not only creates suffering in our lives but has negative effects on our bodies and health as well, causing imbalance and congestion of all kinds. As you open, become sensitive to others, and give of yourself, much pain and limitation dissolve and you become able grow and be free.

CHAPTER 6

# Guarding Your Words: Loshon Hora and the Zen Practice of Silence

*Forty-nine years and not a word said.*
—Book of the Zen Grove

W ORDS HAVE POWER. WE speak to draw closer to others, to be understood, or to dissemble. We can use language to let someone know who we are and how we feel, or to cover up, hide, make a false impression, influence, control, or otherwise manipulate. We can speak to instruct and guide, or to lead astray. Words that are spoken to deceive or disarm, to confuse or discourage raise endless difficulties. Many live with remorse at not being able to take back harsh words they have said. A healthy life and solid relationships are built on trust. You must also be able to trust yourself. Unless you are good to your word, faith and integrity cannot be established. Unless you learn how to live your word and walk your talk, your world and the world of those you interact with will be steeped in chaos.

Both Jewish and Zen practice deal with communication deeply. Jewish practice places great emphasis on words and the effect they have in our lives. Zen practice emphasizes the wordless word we hear during silence. In Zen words can be a block to true communication, used to hide or distract. Zen students focus on other means of expression, which are spontaneous and direct. Words are used in an evocative manner, intending to communicate viscerally, their literal meaning unimportant. But beyond the different emphasis, both practices explore communication to the farthest extent possible.

## Jewish Practice and the Power of Words

Jewish practice places great emphasis on words. They can become a source of blessings or curses, health or depression, inspiration or discouragement. You may not fully realize the power of the words you speak or listen to. What you say and what you take in can come back to haunt you in all kinds of ways. You are strongly warned not to swear deceitfully. Words are to be guarded, used carefully and constructively. Because the word has so much power, certain names in prayers, for instance, are said only at specific times, in specific places. With your words, you can build a world or you can tear it down.

If you stop for a moment and look at your life, it is easy to see how a simple word someone says has the power to disturb you—or give you hope and inspiration. Words are so vital that Jewish practice teaches that if you say something three times it is considered to be a vow. Because words are so powerful, you must be careful to maintain awareness of what you are saying and hearing, as well as refraining from lies, gossip, exaggeration, and deception of all kinds. As you do so, you are observing the mitzvah of *loshon hora*, controlling your tongue and being careful not to do harm. Correct communication does not confuse, give mixed messages, or create fantasies or deception. We cannot find or live the truth unless our communication is clear, both with ourselves and others.

## The Mitzvah of *Loshon Hora*: What Is It?

Guarding your words, or *loshon hora*, is one of the most vital mitzvot in Judaism, one which we have an opportunity to practice all day long. It is said that the Second Jewish Temple was destroyed because the people did not keep *loshon hora*, because they spoke unkindly about one another and gave in to gossip and baseless hatred. In fact, the Chofetz Chaim, a great Jewish teacher of the twentieth century teaches, "A person is credited with a mitzvah every moment he refrains from speaking *loshon hora*."

The mitzvah of *loshon hora* forbids anyone to gossip, slander, insult, deceive, exaggerate, or speak unkindly or dishonestly of another. If you insult someone publicly and he blushes, it is as though you have killed him. Public humiliation of any kind kills a person's self-regard; the person is diminished not only in the eyes of others but in his own eyes as well. It is startling to notice how casually this injunction is disregarded today. It seems easy and natural to go along with gossip and slander of all kinds. Couples often embarrass each other in front of their friends, parents shame children, public figures are routinely deprecated. So many talented people avoid public service for fear of being ripped apart.

The mitzvah of *loshon hora* teaches that when you speak ill of another, not only do you engage in a form of aggression but you have no idea of the wide-ranging consequences. You can destroy a person's reputation, relationships with others, and even livelihood. Beyond that, it is not fair; the person is not present to defend himself. Jewish practice is built on justice.

Unfortunately, it seems to be very difficult to keep this mitzvah. Once I gave this as an exercise to an entire class—to become aware of and stop *loshon hora,* to stop gossiping and listening to gossip for just one week. They came back and reported that it was almost impossible. If they stopped gossiping and listening to gossip, there would be nothing to say, no one to talk to. And what were they to do when someone gossiped to them? What could they say in return?

It is much easier to stop gossiping when you begin to realize how deeply it impacts your life and the life of others. Finding ways out of it is an interesting challenge.

My grandfather Shmuel, my father's father, a full-time Torah scholar, was totally committed to this mitzvah, and had a radical way of observing it: he barely spoke at all. Whenever he visited and anyone said anything in his presence that could be construed as gossip, lies, or exaggeration, he simply held his hand up and said, "*Loshon hora,*" completely putting an end to the conversation. As my mother constantly wanted to read her poems to him and tell him odd stories, his hand was almost always up at our house, and his ears shut most of the time. During his visits, I spent many hours sitting next to him in complete silence. Wherever he went he brought a volume of the Torah with him, had it open, and was always pouring over its words. I don't know if he ever even realized I was sitting there.

There is always the danger of using a mitzvah to shut others down or block out anything you do not want to hear. My mother's poems were not necessarily *loshon hora*, but my grandfather refused to listen to them for fear of hearing something he should not. (This is called putting a fence around a mitzvah: doing it with extra strictness in order to avoid transgressing). It may have also been my grandfather's way of trying to control the situation. Certainly, there was another mitzvah he was missing: to reach out to and love those he cared for.

There is a real balancing act that goes on when you keep a mitzvah, and that is why it is necessary to understand all of its particulars. You need to look at the largest picture. Nothing is to be adhered to blindly. For example, even when it is Sabbath, you are required to break the Sabbath laws if it means saving another person's life. In the Talmud there is intricate discussion of the details of each mitzvah to make sure the highest priorities are always taken into account.

## Zen Practice and Communication

A famous Zen saying goes, "Wash out your mouth before you speak about Zen."

The truth cannot be encompassed in words; whatever you say is off the mark. Words will only confuse the matter, lead the listener astray. Many koans demand that you bring the answer without words. It is too easy to get attached to words, too easy to mistake the finger pointing to the moon with the moon itself. The map is not the territory; words are the map of reality, not the real thing.

Yet we live in a world of words and all of us get caught in beliefs, thoughts, and images. Before we know it, we mistake our ideas *about* reality for what is actually so. We confuse the images we have of someone with the actual person in front of our eyes. This is a root cause of much upset in relationships. After a while, when our initial fantasies and projections fade, we are faced with the reality of the person we are with. This is when trouble often begins.

In my early years in Zen practice, there was someone I totally idealized and adored. In my mind this was the perfect person, someone who fulfilled all I had ever dreamed about. Then quite suddenly, difficulties arose, and I discovered facts about this person I had no idea of before. In deep shock, I could not eat or sleep, could not even do zazen. I felt as if the ground beneath my feet was trembling. At that time, a dear friend and sangha member, Min Pai, said something that allowed me to regain myself and my practice.

"You thought you loved this person so much," Min said to me. "But you didn't. You just loved your fantasies about him. When you really know the entire truth about a person and still love them, then you're really doing something. That's when practice begins."

His words struck deep. I recognized their truth. How much sorrow, distress, and deep anxiety arises because we are attached to an idealized image of a person that has nothing to do with who he or she is. How often we fall in love with our words and images, barely knowing the reality they point to at all. When people say I'm not in love anymore, this usually means that reality has set in, that their illusions about the other person are fading away. Only once these delusions are dissolved is it possible to learn what it means to truly love. Zen practice undoes these delusions, one by one.

## The Zen Practice
## of Dispelling Negativity

Beyond our relationship with others, we have so many ideas about who we are and who we should be, so many idealized self-images. Much self-hatred comes from the discrepancy between an idealized self-image and the reality of who we are. This discrepancy is the fuel for much *loshon hora*, much gossiping, exaggeration, and lies. We are ashamed of the darkness within, reject ourselves because of it, lie, exaggerate, and build a false front. A great amount of our life force then goes to pretending to be someone we aren't. We pretend to be good and holy, while inside us all kinds of negative feelings stir. Yet no matter how much we pretend to be someone we aren't, who we really are comes forth. In order to overcome this dilemma, Sosan, a great Zen teacher, said, "To separate what you like from what you dislike is the disease of the mind." You must stop judging, hating, and rejecting the different aspects of yourself and others. When you are able to do this, the need for *loshon hora* will end.

However, when we reject and suppress our negativity, it accumulates steam and sooner or later erupts, creating physical and mental symptoms, painful relationships, and loneliness. We also project these negative feelings on others and then gossip, slander, lash out, blame others, judge, and condemn them to feel better about ourselves. How is it possible to stop all this? Zen practice teaches that this negativity will dissolve naturally, as we come in touch with our Buddha nature.

## Manifesting Your Buddha Nature

Buddha nature is who we basically are, the part of ourselves that is enlightened, compassionate, and honest. Our Buddha nature is always present, only covered over temporarily by clouds of ignorance, anger, and folly, the afflictions in our lives. The work of zazen is to help these clouds disperse and allow the Buddha nature to shine through. No matter how you presently live or behave, no matter how many dark clouds have gathered, you have the full potential for goodness and enlightenment. Your Buddha nature is right with you, waiting. It is who you truly are.

As you practice, you connect to and live from your Buddha nature. When others come into the zendo, you do not separate those you like from those you dislike. You do not reject or judge people because slowly you grow to see that one moment you may not like someone, while the very next moment, you find something beautiful about her. Good and bad, what you like and dislike, are all passing phenomena that do not express who you truly are. If negative, rejecting thoughts come up, you give them no credence; simply pay no attention to them.

By doing zazen, you take responsibility for all your thoughts and feelings. As you do this, you no longer need to project your negativity on others or onto the world at large. You do not speak about your irritations, dwell on them, or try to change anything. Instead, you simply become aware of what's going on inside and let it go.

This is the practice of making friends with all parts of ourselves. As we make friends with ourselves, inevitably we become a friend to others as well. As we offer acceptance to the difficult parts of ourselves and others, they become able to evolve and grow. It is almost impossible to truly heal relationships, stop gossiping, be truly constructive, or live a fulfilling life until we are willing to become aware of and accept all that goes on within. As we do this, little by little, we stop fighting and hating ourselves and others; we become quiet inside. And then suddenly someone we thought we couldn't stand becomes a close friend.

When I first started at the zendo, about thirty-five years ago, a woman named Sara arrived the same night I did for instruction and was in my preparatory class. For some reason, we couldn't stand each other. Everything she did irritated me. Everything I said drove her crazy. She reminded me of all I couldn't bear, but as both of us loved zazen and came to sit almost daily, there was no way we could avoid each other. So, I was constantly confronted with this person that I would not accept and who would not accept me.

Beyond that, during sesshins (retreats), the seating in our zendo was arranged according to seniority, so the preparatory students were always together. One way or another, Sara and I always ended up being seated next to each other. Once, on our way to sesshin at a monastery in upstate New York, we became particularly irritated with each other. When we got out, Sara, trying to calm things down, placed her palms together and bowed to me, saying, "I bow to the Buddha within you." I thought she was pretentious and didn't like it.

Fed up with the situation, she stormed away and did her best to get the seating changed, but nothing could be done. Once again, we ended up sitting beside each other on the cushion for a full week. As we both went to many sesshins, we had to live through long hours and years of sitting side-by-side, confronting these irritations. We are doomed to be stuck with each other forever, I thought.

Finally she took time off to deal with personal matters. I was so relieved. Then, unexpectedly, months later, I was having lunch in an out of the way restaurant downtown, and she walked in. We were startled to see one another and ran to greet one another with great joy. It was as if I were greeting a long lost sister. I had no idea how much I'd missed her.

"Here you are," she hugged me, delighted. "I'd felt part of me was gone."

From that time on, we were best friends, and for the next five years I was with her during many life situations that arose. Despite the initial friction between us, our Buddha nature had grown. When it was strong enough, the irritations of the past dissolved into the sun.

Then, from out of nowhere, came Sara's surprising illness and sudden burial. As she was dying, she thanked me for being her sitting partner for the past twenty years and asked me to help with funeral arrangements. Before I knew it, I stood at the burial grounds, the same monastery where we had practiced together all these years. I stood alongside our Zen Master, the monks and nuns, friends, Sara's children and family, who brought her ashes to be interred. Our Zen Master chanted powerfully as the early summer sun slanted through the trees, making odd shadows on the ground. What were all those years of struggle between us, I wondered, as I watched her ashes being placed in the soil.

After the service, tea and cookies were served in the small house near the lake. Our Zen Master joined and turned to me and said, "Eshin, you are a good friend." I never forgot that. It was one of the only times he ever praised me. And it was enough; to be a good friend was everything. To this day, many years later, I still feel Sara at times, sitting beside me on the cushion.

## The Jewish Practice
### of *Loshon Hora*

Jewish practice dispels negativity in a different way. You put an end to *loshon hora* by taking control of both what you say and what you listen to. You guard your tongue and do not allow habitual responses to run your life. Sometimes it is more difficult to hold your tongue at a tense moment than to sit in zazen for many hours. Sitting in zazen for hours helps greatly, though, when these tense moments come. Beyond speaking ill of another, you must not *listen* to gossip, lies, insults, and slander. Another person cannot indulge in gossip if you refuse to listen. Torah teaches that that if you inadvertently hear *loshon hora*, you should immediately tell yourself that it is not true. Create constructive doubt about it. Give the other person the benefit of the doubt. Find positive explanations for the negative behavior that is being described. As you do so, you protect your own mind from plunging into judgment and condemnation, and you help others as well.

In order to practice *loshon hora* carefully, you must learn specifics connected with it. It is important to be aware of the different situations you find yourself in, so you will know how and when to respond. There are situations in which it is important to speak ill of another. If you know something about someone that could cause harm to another, then you are required to warn the individual who could be harmed. If you do not, and if this individual is harmed as a result, you are responsible for the pain she suffers. For example, if you know that

Lou dates women for a short period and then leaves them for someone new, and your friend is starting to date him, you have a responsibility to let her know this; what she does then is up to her; you have done what you could to prevent future harm.

When you do not allow negative thoughts about others to run amok, you are also guarding yourself from the experience of paranoia, which is built on suspicion of others. A paranoid person projects his unconscious negativity onto others and so deeply believes the dark stories in his mind, he often cannot let even a little light in, or see anything positive. He then becomes largely unable to see the facts before his eyes. Paranoia is an extreme form of *loshon hora*, indulging in negative slander and gossip within one's own mind.

A wonderful story told by the Chabad Hasidim illustrates the great importance of tending to your speech. Rabbi Israel Baal Shem Tov, the founder of the Hasidic movement, once instructed several of his disciples to embark on a journey. The Hasidic leader did not tell them where to go, nor did they ask. They allowed divine providence to direct their wagon where it may, confident that the destination and purpose of their trip would be revealed. The Baal Shem Tov and his disciples were pious Jews who insisted on the highest standards of kashrut (laws of eating kosher food). When they arrived and learned that their host planned to serve them meat, they interrogated him in great detail to make sure the meat was fit to be eaten. As they spoke and ate, a voice emerged from behind the oven, where an old beggar was resting amid his bundles. "Dear Jews," the beggar called out, "are you as careful with what comes out of your mouth as you are with what enters into it?"

The Hasidim concluded their meal in silence. They now understood why their Rebbe had sent them on their journey.

## Practicing *Loshon Hora* Today

In our modern-day technological world, it is easy to feel disenfranchised and insignificant, as if we were no more than a cog in a wheel. The mitzvah of *loshon hora* tells us otherwise. It shows how powerful our smallest actions are, how each person we come into contact with is someone we impact deeply, either positively or negatively. As we realize this, our sense of purpose increases and our life no longer feels random. Guarding our words also forces us to stop dwelling on the shortcomings of others. Instead, we must focus on what is positive, meaningful, and uplifting about them. This itself has the power to heal relationships and turn many aspects of your life around. *Loshon hora* is a mitzvah that creates a world where each person looks out for the benefit of the other. And as you do that, the gates of your heart open wide.

## Remaining Positive
## Through Difficult Times

All true spiritual practice comes to help us find a positive, constructive way through difficult times. But how do we remain positive and constructive when negative communication comes at us, when we are insulted, abused, treated unfairly, or when feelings of hurt or betrayal arise? Throughout the history of Zen, Masters consistently berated and insulted their students to teach them how to handle difficult times. It was also a way of diminishing ego, dismantling a false sense of importance, and breaking the leaning, depending mind. When you have the experience of being shocked, hurt, betrayed, with nothing to turn to or lean on, it is then that you can find the deepest strength within. Of course, this experience can also be so devastating that you feel you cannot go on. Wisdom is needed here.

## Dissolving Negative Karma

Normally, when we are hurt or insulted, we feel justified in lashing back, thinking the person's behavior gives us the right to do so. However, in Zen practice, no matter what happens, we learn to remain firmly planted in our center and fully be with whatever is going on. Then whatever response we make will be appropriate to the occasion and come from a different part of ourselves. It will not come as a form of revenge or another negative impulse.

Zen practice teaches that whatever happens arises from seeds you have planted at one time or another. Difficult times have been created by karma of your own making. Karma refers to thoughts, deeds, desires, and feelings that have been habitual in your life (and past lives as well). When these run automatically, they inevitably create consequences. What you sow, you shall reap. If you have dwelled on thoughts and deeds of anger, negative situations return in response. When you choose to turn this around, your karma lessens and alters as well.

This does not mean you should blame yourself when difficult times arise. Instead, it is empowering to understand that whatever seeds you sow will sooner or later yield fruit. By receiving the fruits of past karma now, not only can you learn from it, but past negativity can be rebalanced. There are no victims—only lessons. You learn these lessons well when you do not respond in kind.

Difficult karma, a turbulent inner and outer life, can actually become a blessing when it becomes fuel for practice. One early morning in the zendo, I was doing zazen, when suddenly Soen Roshi came quickly down the aisle, stopped behind me, and whispered in my ear, "Bad karma relations, good dharma relations." Then he moved on.

I was stunned. I sat with that for a very long while, realizing that the bad karma, the pain and obstacles I struggled with, were blessings in disguise if I used them properly. They had come into my life to stimulate me to practice, to become awake and compassionate and live a fuller life. A teaching recited at morning service describes this perfectly:

> *If by any chance a friend should turn against us*
> *And become a sworn enemy*
> *And abuse and persecute us,*
> *We should sincerely bow down with humble language*
> *In the reverent belief that he is*
> *The merciful avatar of Buddha*
> *Who uses devices to emancipate us*
> *From sinful karma*
> *That has been produced and accumulated*
> *Upon ourselves*
> *By our own egoistic delusion and a*
> *Through the countless cycles of our being*

## Turning Negativity into a Blessing

The Jewish concept of karma is called tikkun—which means a fixing, a correction, or healing of our souls. Jewish teachings tell us that we have come into this world to correct, rebalance, and fix parts of ourselves. Tikkun olam means healing and fixing the entire world. Jewish practice also teaches that painful events come for a reason: to balance past negativity and teach us to grow. The correct way to deal with abuse is to turn it into a blessing. The Torah says, "If someone abuses you verbally, just remain silent and rejoice. Do not insist on your rights, be ready to receive hurt without response. Instead, say to yourself, 'God brought it about that this person would do this to me in order to atone for my sins, if I receive the blow with humility and love of God.'"

Both Zen and Jewish practice teach that any pain, difficulty, and abuse you receive comes to clear past errors and remove pride. When you respond correctly to these events, they have the power to elevate you and clear darkness away. Of course it is difficult to respond positively unless you see the larger picture about why the difficulty has come. If you do not understand or cannot see a positive purpose in your suffering, then it is natural to respond negatively and intensify the difficulty you're in. However, if you receive the hard time quietly, even pray for forgiveness for the one who has done the harm, you will grow spiritually and bring light to the world.

## The Jewish Practice
## of Blessing Others

The Torah says, "If someone curses you, answer with the blessing, 'Peace be upon you.'" Beyond responding quietly to negative speech, you are to go one step further and actually respond positively. We are told to offer blessings, which transform pain into healing. Just as it is a great mitzvah not to gossip or speak ill of others, it is an equal mitzvah to use language to bless. In fact, blessings are a daily, vital part of Jewish practice. You are to make blessings all day long; bless the food you eat, the people you interact with, sunsets, moments of beauty, even events like seeing someone you haven't seen for a while.

Bless difficult times and situations, including the death or loss of a loved one. As you offer blessings you not only affirm the best in others, but bring the best out in them. What you bless increases and strengthens.

When you arise, first thing in the morning, you are to wash your hands, wash away lingering debris, and start the day fresh and new. Then you make many blessings. These blessings set the course of your day. As you bless others, you are blessed as well. The very first blessing is Modeh Ani, thanking and praising God for returning your soul to your body, to live another day. Beyond blessings that are made routinely in the morning, many more blessings are listed in the prayer book (siddur). For example, when you see a person you have not see for a long time, you say, "Blessed is he who comes in the name of God."

This practice is not just for Jews. Whether you are aware of it or not, the way you use your thoughts, words, and deeds becomes a source of blessings or curses to those with whom you come in contact. When you use language in a focused, positive manner, it becomes a means of maintaining awareness of God in all situations. If you consistently do this, you will decrease illness, pain, and misunderstanding in your life and the lives of others. Plain conversation then becomes a form of worship, a way to constantly remember God.

## The Practice of Communion:
## Inner and Outer Silence

Words are one kind of communication. Though they carry power, we can go even deeper, into the communion that takes place during silence. In fact, true communication begins when all words have ceased. True communication turns to communion, not only with the one spoken to, but with the very Source of Life.

In his book *Between Man and Man* Martin Buber tells the story of a time he was a passenger on a train. He was sitting next to a stranger as the train traveled along. Suddenly the normal reserve that both of them held themselves in lifted, and pure communication silently streamed back and forth. Although not a word was said, both were gripped in another level of connection. Pure communion took place. Buber said it was as if they knew everything about one another and shared deepest truths. This connection and understanding was deeper and more satisfying and penetrating than anything that might have transpired had words been spoken. Through the silence all was known.

Many of us have experienced moments when our usual way of being with another person alters, our defenses dissolve, and we no longer experience the other as someone separate from us, but instead connect with the deepest humanity which unites us both. At moments like this, oneness, or communion, is experienced, and in that state all is known. This experience is, in many ways, the heart of Zen practice. The silence in zazen is not withdrawal, but the process of opening up and becoming available, releasing the walls we normally live behind. This silence not only dissolves negativity but becomes a source of deep well-being. Not only does it reach out and touch others, but it stops the compulsion to present a false front, lie, or hide from the truth. When you do speak, your language arises from a different place where your words can become a blessing to all.

## Different Kinds of Silence

Silence too, however, can be used for different purposes. There is the cold silence in a relationship when a person withholds or withdraws. There is the silence of uncertainty and fear, when an individual is afraid to express himself. There is the silence of anger where guilt is being produced. Although you are silent, your silence often speaks more forcefully than your words ever could.

As you engage in ongoing practice, a deeper silence emerges. It comes by itself. This silence can be called *samadhi*. It has also been called "the peace that passeth understanding," the holy spirit, or nirvana. It is a silence that comes over your mind and heart and lets you know that, no matter what happens, all is well. It also lets you know that we are all branches on the same tree. You do not need to hunt, grab, cling, or damage another vine or view other branches as enemies. There is always enough sap in the tree for all. When you are in that deeper silence, it is easy to see that every part of life is a precious gift.

## Guidelines to Jewish Practice

Below are several exercises that will start you on the path of healing and empowering your communication and also making you more open and available to the communication of others. Some of these exercises will be more suitable and meaningful. Try them all at least once and then work with those that speak most to you.

### STOPPING *LOSHON HORA*

Describe in writing the times you remember speaking ill of someone. Also write down times when you flattered, deceived, exaggerated, or lied. This is not to create guilt but to open up your awareness. Keep a journal of what happens as you practice each day.

Decide that for one day, and one day only, you will go on a fast from gossip. You will not listen either. If you happen to hear gossip inadvertently, make note. Don't just let it pass. This is a practice of mindfulness, of preventing you from falling into automatic patterns.

Give up lying and exaggerating today. If you notice yourself starting to do so, stop it on the spot. Even if you can't fully stop, just noticing that you are doing it is a fine step.

## CORRECTING PAST NEGATIVITY

Needless to say, we all have been involved in past negativity. You may wonder how to wipe the slate clean, how to erase whatever damage may have occurred and prevent it from happening again.

Sincerely regret what you have done.

Admit it and resolve not to repeat it again.

If the listener believed the gossip and the person was harmed in any way by it, request forgiveness from the person who suffered. Tell him about what you have said and ask for forgiveness.

## EMPOWERING YOUR SPEECH

Along with blessings, here are some practices that allow you to empower your speech, elevate yourself, and bring inspiration and healing to all.

Say at least one blessing a day.

During all speech and conversation, maintain an awareness of God.

When you talk to people, feel as though you are talking to, or in front of, God.

Whatever you happen to hear said to you, receive those words as if they were messages to you from God.

When talking with another person, consider it as if you are talking with yourself. What would you want to hear?

## The Zen Practice of Silence

Silence can be actively practiced. It is not the absence of noise but the presence of awareness and acceptance. Trungpa Rimpoche describes it this way: "We cannot stop the noise, but we can stop ourselves. We can accept the noise."

As you grow more aware of your inner chaos, more willing to be the silent observer and let it go, you will be not be empowering your negativity. Then silence will come all by itself.

Decide to be quiet today, to speak only when needed.

Omit all superficial chatter.

Watch what goes on in your mind as you quiet your outer actions.

See what is unacceptable to you in relationships; make a list. See what causes upset and defensiveness in yourself. Take one item a day and see if just for that day, you can accept it. Just let it be as it is. Appreciate it. As you do so, you will quiet down deeply within.

If you can, spend fifteen minutes or more sitting in zazen, either in a chair or on the floor. Doing so will help you to begin the journey toward real silence.

# CHAPTER 7

# Finding True Support: Dissolving False Attachments and Letting Go

*If anyone by form seeks me, By voice seeks me,*
*Wrongly turned are his footsteps on the way.*
— DIAMOND SUTRA

A S WE SEARCH IN life for that which will truly support and sustain us it is easy to be misled. Many spend hours in the gym and depend on their bodies for a sense of well-being and strength. Becoming attached to their physical prowess, they base their sense of security on that which must inevitably change and weaken. While physical well-being is wonderful, when it is turned to for basic strength and support, sooner or later it will let you down.

In the same way, others turn to relationships, work, education, beauty, or money for support or to save them from difficulty. However, conditions constantly change, and those who rely on relationships, work, money, or beauty will also discover that they have been putting their trust in something that can never ultimately provide the support and well-being needed. When they wake up to the truth of the matter and discover they have been going down a blind alley, they are left feeling emptier than before. It can take a long while to discover what to trust, where to turn in a time of need, what it is that can never let you down.

The question of where to put our faith is the bedrock on which all spiritual practices are based. It is the search for the fundamental basis of life, a place where we can come to balance and rest. Both Jewish and Zen practice warn us continually about depending on something that cannot be trusted. Zen insists that we take our attachment away from the external world and become planted deeply within. Jewish practice teaches to turn to God and depend only on God. We must take power away from all the false idols we create and bow down to that do not have the power to heal or save.

## Jewish Practice and Idol Worship

In the present day, no one thinks about idol worship. Most people do not think they worship anything, least of all idols. But you can be said to worship whatever you put your trust in, what you turn to in time of need. Is it money, financial stability or independence, status, degrees, accomplishments, relationships? Or do you worship yourself, spend hours and fortunes building up your ego? All of these only bring passing security and cannot be depended on; they are considered to be false idols.

*Avodah zorah* is the command not to worship idols or to have false gods. This mitzvah is such a powerful part of Judaism that it is repeated on almost every page of the Torah, in one form or another. It says, "Do not turn to idols. Do not make for yourself a graven image, or anything that has the likeness of a human. Do not bow down to it." Over and over you are reminded of this. Not only is it considered one of the gravest mistakes, but it is ultimately a form of slavery.

This particular mitzvah is what stopped me from going forward along the traditional Zen path. When it came time in the zendo to bow down in front of the statues of Buddha, I thought of the command, "Do not worship idols," and stood there frozen, while everyone else was bowed to the ground. There are many ways of explaining and justifying the bowing that could have made it acceptable: it was simply bowing to the awakened mind, it was surrendering ego or revering the dharma, the truth of life. These were all beautiful teachings, but nevertheless, I did not bow. I kept standing often right beside my Zen Master as he bowed to the ground. Fortunately, in all these years, he never said a word to me about it and I am eternally grateful to him for that. Tacitly, he understood. Now, in the zendo in my home we have no statues and nobody bows. We also have no teacher, and no one gives any teachings. If people come, they come. If they have to go, they go. We just sit, offer blessings and prayers, and when the times come, study both Zen teachings and Torah. My heart is at ease.

## Come to Me Only

Jewish practice teaches not to attribute power to anything to save you but God. You are not permitted to pray to anything that has a form. God is formless and cannot be known through the senses. You must not bow down to that which has been created, or worship and adore the work of your hands. If you worship that which is visible, sooner or later, you will become enslaved by it; in the end it will come to nothing, and you will not receive true support.

The command not to worship idols is written on almost every page of the Torah because we all have such a deep need for comfort, strength, and reassurance. We have a deep tendency to become attached to that which we can see, hear, smell, taste, and touch. It is easy to feel that what our senses show us is the entire world. Jewish practice says this is not so. There are worlds upon worlds we have no awareness of. When we refuse to worship idols and follow only God, not only will our awareness of other dimensions increase, but our lives will prosper and we will be healed.

Idol worship is so dangerous because, in essence, it is a denial of our basic purpose in this world: to become unified with God and his will. The practice of idol worship scatters our forces and promotes the delusion that there are forces or beings other than God to be worshiped or feared. In this way, the power of God is lessened in our minds and we are trapped by that which we have turned to. Following the will of God is all that is needed for complete strength, protection, and fulfillment.

Many object to this strongly, saying that an image or a statue is simply a pointer, something that inspires them, elevates their consciousness, or helps them remember God. This is completely different from worship. In reply, the Torah states that it is very easy to rationalize behavior, and also to start with one intention and get pulled into something else. It's natural to start by viewing an image of a person as reminder of God, and then, before you know it, associate the two and become overly attached to the person. You then start idealizing a human being in ways that are to be reserved only for God.

Idealization and worship of teachers happens all over the place. We have all seen gurus or preachers being venerated in this manner and how dependency on them grows, interfering with their students' judgment and ability to stand on their own. Too many of these gurus and preachers then become swept away by their own self-importance and use this power ruthlessly. We have responsibility for this as well. We have given them the trust and power that should be reserved only for God. Observing the mitzvah of idol worship protects us from this confusion and the negative consequences that follow.

In the beginning of my practice of zazen, I did not worry about idol worship. I didn't worry about anything. Soen Roshi said over and over that Zen is a practice, not a religion, and I just returned to the beautiful wooden zendo and sat there every day. As months went by, Reb Bershky was replaced in my mind by my beautiful Zen Master, in whom all my questions seemed to find a perfect home. I listened to him for my very life. This was no easy job for him either, trying to bring reality to each of the students who saw him through the lens of their own particular dreams.

"There are many pitfalls in the practice of Zen," my Zen Master would warn. "It is easy to become confused and fall. But a good student learns how to get up quickly again."

I sat straighter.

"The universe as we know it is not the way it appears to be. It is a flash of lightning, a dewdrop only. Thus it is to be regarded. Do you understand?"

Although we all thought we understood, nobody did.

He continued anyway, "It does not matter what you do or do not understand, just keep working with your koan. Once you become enlightened, then not only you but five generations of your family will become free."

Five generations of my family? I could hardly suppress the joy that rose. A sudden picture of my grandmother Devorah popped into my mind. I saw her with her big wig on, her body covered, endlessly moving about in her white kitchen. I heard the words she always said, "Who is left to help the Jewish people? Who knows how to really try? Tell me, where can you find a real Jew?"

I look over at my Japanese Zen Master. Grandma, I longed to whisper to her, could it be possible that I found someone who knows how to really try? That I found a real Jew at last? Could you ever understand?

But my Zen Master's voice interrupted the reveries that went on relentlessly within. "Perhaps it might seem like a strange thing to talk about the generations of our families and about death on this beautiful spring afternoon, when new life is about to bloom. But please remember, there is no spring without winter, no life without death. One generation passes so another can come. We too must die to the old to allow the new to be born. Without the cold death of winter, how can the spring come?"

I thought of the spring back in Borough Park, of the few bluebells that struggled for air, and of the garden my grandmother always planted full of purple and yellow irises.

My Zen Master's words went deep inside, but as I thought of home, little by little, the words of the Torah rose to counter them. It was as though I could hear Reb Bershky replying, "All

Jews are commanded not to forget, to always remember. Observe and remember, it's a single command. It's forbidden to bow before a statue. It's forbidden to revere a man. This is considered the worst sin of all. All through history Jews have given up their lives, rather than do this. How about you?"

I had no answer, just sat more deeply.

After many months of practicing like this, one morning after zazen, I was invited to go upstairs and have breakfast with my teacher and a few students. Sheila, a beautiful, gentle resident at the zendo, tapped my shoulder lightly. "Please join us," she said and smiled brightly.

Upstairs, we all sat silently on the floor around a long wooden table, unpacked little eating bowls, and filled them with a breakfast of oatmeal, peanuts, and warm milk. After eating in silence, we washed our bowls and wrapped them up again. Then all got up and went together into the meeting room to sit in a circle on the floor and have a cup of tea.

"And where are you from?" my Zen Master asked me simply and directly, as I was sipping my green tea.

All eyes turned to me. At first I wanted to say from Brooklyn, but I just looked up at him and smiled. He smiled back for a moment. In that split moment we recognized each other, compatriots, warriors, ancient companions. And in that moment I realized that he would not make it easy for me; he could not, did not dare. For a sword to grow strong and worthy, it had to be tested in many fires.

"Where are you from?" he asked more pointedly.

"Nowhere at all," I replied.

He made a funny face. "Really?" Everyone laughed, and I laughed too.

"Where are you from?" he boomed more loudly then, an edge of anger in his tone.

"Here."

"Where?"

"Here."

"You must sit more," he said then, rather kindly. "It's imperative!"

"I will."

"Good."

Then Sheila poured us all another cup of tea.

"Do your best," the Zen Master demanded, "your very best."

I'm trying, I whispered to myself. Believe me, I'm finally learning what it really means to try.

Before long, Soen Roshi visited once again from Japan. I was given a dharma name, Eshin. "Eshin means wisdom and faith," Soen Roshi said. "A name to grow into. It could take hundreds of years. Or it could happen just like that!"

What could happen? I was bewildered. Everyone here had the constant feeling that anything could happen, everything was possible. And it was. I came to discover endless surprises over the years, both in my life and in the lives of others there. Some of these surprises were wonderful, others disturbing. But the practice itself taught us how to be with all that came, both the bitter and the sweet. We were not to reject, judge, or run from difficult conditions, but to continue sitting, see through all circumstances, and move forward bravely, no matter what.

"During zazen," my Zen Master informed us, "everything that is within comes up to be seen. It comes up to be digested. This does not happen consciously, but it happens nevertheless. Be very careful. Do not get caught."

He was right, but questions still haunted me. As zazen deepened, I could not avoid the persistent questions that rose up within—I thought about my family, cousins, parents, sister, brother. Am I abandoning you, I wondered? Have I left my Jewish roots behind? Am I running away from who I truly am? What about all those who died to uphold the Torah? At certain times I felt that doing deep zazen, I was fulfilling the true Torah, actualizing all the commandments. Other times, dressed in my Zen robes, I felt as though I was trespassing, violating my deepest self.

One day I went to speak with my Zen Master about it directly. "Idol worship . . ." I began.

"The Buddha statue is not an idol." His answer was sharp and quick. "It is a reminder of balanced mind and body."

But the words of Reb Bershky rose to the surface, "Torah is the only medicine, do not look to the left or to the right. Do not get lost on strange pathways. False gods you are worshiping, and there will be a price to pay for it. "

Of course my Zen Master saw my trouble. He also saw that he could do nothing about it. "We are karma beings," he said, trying once more to help. "Just sit more, Eshin. Your zazen will melt this torment away."

I tried. Months went by, but nothing lasts, how could it? The time of intense practice and concentration, the beauty, clarity, and silence I had found, was being endangered. Seriously endangered. But danger was fine, my Zen Master had told us. "Real practice includes everything. Times of great calm and turbulence too. You can't have one without the other. Practice comes in every way."

"Sit," he kept urging me. "Eshin, sit. Do zazen."

But now it became harder to hear him. " One day I said to him, I feel I should go home."

"Where is your true home?"

I breathed deeply for a moment.

"Your true home. Before you were born! Eshin, calm down. You have not done wrong. You are not doing wrong here."

"According to my people I must go home."

"Then stop coming."

"I can't."

"Then sit more deeply, to the very bottom of the well. Finally, when you are ripe, you will see that we are all One."

## Zen Practice and the Nature of Delusion

In Zen practice we grow to see that life is a constant process of fluctuation, happiness and unhappiness, hope and disappointment, coming and going, gain and loss. What you counted on yesterday changes drastically today. What seemed as if it would last forever is here for a moment and then gone. What you once believed in so fervently suddenly seems unacceptable as your eyes are opened to new aspects of that belief. Although we cling to familiar anchors that provide temporary comfort, it is necessary to let false anchors go in order to find true, lasting support. Zen practice teaches that the feeling that everything will stay the same, that change will never come, is the very nature of all delusion. Life does change. We lose our possessions. Our partner goes away, our hair gets thin. We try to pretend this isn't happening, try to keep everything the same. Yet no matter how desperately we try to hold everything together, everything constantly transforms. The Diamond Sutra, a basic text of

Zen, states this clearly: "All compounded things must necessarily separate. And thus you must regard this fleeting world, a bubble, a dewdrop, a flash of lightning, a dream on a summer night, it is thus to be regarded."

Life is not to be grasped and used; it is to be lived thoroughly, tasted, experienced, and appreciated. It is a gift you receive, day by day. The more you try to cling to your life (and the people in it), the more you crush whatever you hold in the palm of your hand. The more you resist the changes that are upon you and demand that things stay the same, the more intense your suffering becomes. One of the deepest causes of suffering is attachment—holding on to something that must go. Yet, despite this, most people still feel that their security comes only from holding on, trying to keep things intact.

## The Nature of Attachment

Why do we attach so tenaciously? What creates this kind of response? It seems so automatic, so natural and fundamental that we do not question it at all. Attachment is usual but not natural. Certainly it is not necessary. It arises out of deep confusion about who we truly are, the nature of relationships, and a fear of being abandoned.

We come into life empty-handed and then expect to grab and hold on to everything. Immediately we make claim for ownership, "This is my toy, this is my bottle, this is my mother. She can't go away." Some enormous hunger begins to develop. First it is just food and love that we demand. In the beginning it may be easy to find satisfaction. But soon this craving grows more subtle. Our so-called needs become more intricate.

There are many kinds of foods we require as we grow: emotional food, intellectual, social, and spiritual food. The journey of our lives may be said to be discovering the different kinds of foods we need, how to take them, use, digest, and absorb them. And then how to let go. We cannot keep eating forever. We must learn to be satisfied and let go.

But we want everything and we want it forever. We want to receive, hold, and possess. A child feels his toys belong only to him. This attitude can be hard to outgrow. When change comes, it is seen as a villain that takes our goodies away. But what do we own? What really belongs to us? Even our bodies have a life of their own. We take in many wonderful things, but what are we willing to return to the universe? Certainly not those we love.

Many people center their lives around accumulation, and inevitably along with that the process of attachment appears. Everything seems precious, no matter what. It is not so easy to clean out the drawers. We may not yet have learned the value of empty space. But this clinging is the very core of the pain we experience. It is resistance to the flow of life. If we open our hands and let go, we can easily find our true source of strength and comfort, where our true security lies.

### Nonattachment

The antidote to grasping is nonattachment. This does not mean becoming cold or disconnected from others; just the opposite. Only after you let go are you free to experience gratitude, warmth, and compassion. Only then do you stop trying to twist others into a mold, imagining they exist in order to make you safe and secure. Only then do you stop making people and relationships into idols of all kinds.

A Zen teaching tells us that we are all fish swimming in water while dying of thirst. All are seeking nourishment and safety, while in the midst of it. The entire work of Zen practice is to get you to see that you're in the midst of water. The more you seek it elsewhere, the more you cling to bubbles that burst, the thirstier you will become. As your practice ripens, you do not cling to passing phenomena. Instead, you realize that you are one with the ocean. When that happens, false attachments fade. There is no need to cling to anything. You always have everything you need, as does everyone else.

## The Basic Forms of Idol Worship

In Jewish practice, in order to let go of false attachments, you are instructed to follow the mitzvah of idol worship carefully. In many ways idol worship is a radical mitzvah. Particularly in this day and age, it interferes with many of our usual activities and assumptions.

In the Talmud we are told specifically what idol worship consists of and how to avoid it. This mitzvah is so important that the first thirty-eight negative mitzvot (which we are to refrain from doing) are all concerned with it. We may be surprised to learn that some of the actions we are to refrain from doing, which are considered to be idol worship, are widespread today. No one thinks anything of them, much less that they could be damaging. (These actions will be described in detail below.) Some of the basic instructions about how to observe the mitzvah of idol worship follow, with a brief explanation.

*Do not make any carved idols for yourself. Do not make gods of metal, silver, or gold.* (Do not become attached to anything in form. Do not become hypnotized by all that glitters and shines.) You are not to carve statues, draw pictures, or create any other forms, images, or shapes that will be used for the purpose of worship. God must not be represented in any way.

You are also warned not to make idols of gold, silver, and metals—or other products of the world. This is a warning against being hypnotized and captured by all that glitters in the world. This can refer to diamonds, jewelry, cars, homes, whatever is adored other than God.

*Do not bow down to idols. Do not worship them.* (Do not give power to anything but God.) When you give anything power over your life, feel you cannot do without it, put it above your reliance on God, this is a form of bowing down to an idol.

*Do not utter or listen to false prophecy.* (Do not get caught by false teachings.) False prophecy, a cousin of idol worship, is rampant these days in many forms, causing confusion and blindness. Numberless gurus, psychics, and preachers appear with different messages, signs, systems of enlightenment, or warnings of catastrophes. Some people run from one to another, hoping to gain ease of heart, bliss, or enlightenment. Others stay with one teacher but never look close at how this person is affecting their life, or the lives of others. They do not examine their teacher's behavior, motives, lifestyle, and charismatic posturing.

When someone uses charismatic powers, Torah warns that you should be on guard. Moses, the greatest prophet, was chosen by God because he was the humblest of men. This is the Torah standard: is the person humble and plain? Is he direct and honest in his dealings? Is his life praiseworthy, is he kind? From a Torah perspective, many of today's teachers and preachers, although they may seem charming and well intentioned, fall under the Torah classification of false prophets. Following these individuals can lead to dangers of all kinds.

Torah clearly states that there will be a time when false prophecy will spread all over the world, creating confusion and turning you from the true way. As you follow a false teacher, you can waste years of your life, devotion and inspiration, and end up being derailed.

*There must be found among you no one who practices divination.* (Do not go to those who predict the future.) Today many have a great hunger (and addiction) to knowing the future and regularly consult psychics, astrologers, and mediums. The Torah advises against this. The future is always only in the hands of God. Your responsibility is to turn to God and lead a life that is whole, healing, and worthy of acclaim. Then the future will naturally bring what is good, right, and fulfilling.

When you stop trying to find out about the future, you are also protected from believing false reports and waiting for something to happen which may never come to pass. Instead, you take the necessary actions to make your future what you wish it to be. Beyond that, when you act in accordance with Torah, your relationship with God places you beyond the control of nature, stars, planets, people, and random forces.

*Do not turn to mediums.* (Do not try to contact the dead.) It is only natural to want to establish contact with a loved one who has passed away. But in Jewish practice, attempts to communicate with the dead are not permitted as this can lead into a huge quagmire of fantasy, hopes, and dependency on individuals who say they can accomplish this. Trying to contact the dead is a disruption of the natural order. Sometimes spontaneous dreams of loved ones who have passed away come naturally. This is fine. The spirits of the departed are also said to come close to the living at certain times. They are closer during the Jewish holidays and the anniversary of their death (yahrzeit). The way to communicate at those times is through prayer, Torah study, giving charity in the deceased's name, and performing mitzvot on his or her behalf.

## Zen Practice and Idol Worship

Although it may not seem so on the surface, in essence Zen practice is a repudiation of idol worship. Rather than worship anything in form or become attached to the external world, we are told to take our hands off the world, allow it to go its natural way. We accept whatever is brought to us and engage wholeheartedly with life's natural demands.

In Zen practice no one tries to predict the future or alter circumstances. We are told over and over, the future is not here, stay fully in the present, be with life as it is. Do not seek to discover or manipulate that which lies ahead.

A well-known Zen teaching tells us, "Do not put a head on your head. What is wrong with your own head anyway?" You take back authority from all external forms of knowledge, all appearances, delusions, and beliefs and become present to the wisdom living within.

You do not need to contact those who have died because you do not feel separate from them, wherever they may be.

You understand about life and death, know where you are going, and what to do during your time here. Suzuki Roshi, who was one of the first Japanese Zen Masters to come to America and was the founding Roshi of San Francisco Zen Center, puts this beautifully, "Our life and our death are the same thing. When we realize this fact, we have no fear of death anymore, nor actual difficulty in our life." Suzuki Roshi is pointing to the fact that Zen practice is about discovering the truth about life and death. Rather than escape into ideas and fantasies about life and death, or try to call back those who have departed, we face our experience of both life and death directly. As we do so, one day we see what death truly is. As we do so, we simultaneously see what life truly is, and we become free to live fully.

## Bowing to One Another

The practice of bowing takes place in different forms and for many reasons. Sometimes there is bowing in front of a statue. From the Zen student's point of view, they are not bowing to worship a statue, but to honor and to surrender to the teachings. You need not do this if it feels disturbing. In another form of bowing, called gassho, the hands are brought together and a slight bow is made from the waist, usually to another person, or to the zendo, cushions, tree, sky, or anything that elicits appreciation. This is a way of saying thank-you, recognizing and giving honor to that which you bow to.

For many, bowing is an important part of practice. They say it develops a humble, open state of mind. Suzuki Roshi emphasized bowing practice. "Bowing is a very serious practice," he said. "You should be prepared to bow, even in your last moment. Even though it is impossible to get rid of our self-centered desires, we have to do it. Our true nature wants us to."

Years ago I taught a group of New York City transit authority policemen a class on self-change. These were tough guys who'd seen the worst of life, and to my great surprise, they loved the class and jumped right in, especially the section on Zen. I showed them how to do zazen, even took them to the zendo for beginner instruction on a Thursday night. But to my amazement, the part that was most meaningful to them was the section on bowing—not prostrating to the ground, but putting their hands together and making a small bow (gassho) to the one in front of them. We talked about it in the class that followed, they said it was easy to do and made them feel good. I suggested they do it wherever they were. Before they arrested someone they could bow to that person in their mind. In that moment, they would be acknowledging their common humanity and perhaps be prevented from inadvertently treating the person too harshly. Two of the policemen in the class especially loved the idea. They came back and reported that they tried it, and things turned around. One of them actually felt kindly toward the guy being arrested and that the person was easier to be with as well.

He said, "After I bowed to this guy in my mind, he calmed down and looked at me funny. There was a real person there. I can't get over it. How come?"

Of course the real person was always there, it was only that his stopping and bowing, his taking the moment to be with this person differently, allowed him to see what was in front of his eyes. I then suggested that they all keep doing it and extend it to others as well. They should bow in their minds to family, friends, someone they were about to get into a fight with. See what happened then.

One policeman reported to me that he did it consistently, and that this simple practice had great power in his life. I learned that he went on to get a master's degree in Buddhist studies and became a student of Zen. When we bow to someone in that manner, we are not worshiping him or her as an idol, but recognizing, uniting in, and honoring the Buddha nature that is common to all.

As the disparate parts of our personalities are accepted and united in Zen practice, we become wholehearted and sincere. We stop fighting and asserting our own will in opposition to others. This process can also be called surrender to "what is," or "the will of God." When this happens, not only do we free those around us but become free from manipulation and idols of all kinds. Living in this manner, it is easy to see where our true support lies.

## The Practice of Jewish Meditation

Interestingly enough, a wonderful antidote to idol worship in Jewish practice is Jewish meditation. It places our focus on God and helps us let go of our attachment to people and things, and to the passing worries of the day. One of the greatest sages of ancient times, Shimon ben Gamliel, said, "I grew up among the Sages, all my life I listened to their words. Yet, I have found nothing better for the soul, than silence." Jewish meditation takes us into silence in an active way.

There are many forms of Jewish meditation and to explore them all is beyond the scope of this book. Some meditations work with the Hebrew letters, others with visualizations, some with statements to absorb and dwell on, others with talking to God. All of them cause us to cling to God more deeply *(devekut)* and let go of obsession and grasping in the world.

A few basic, fundamental meditations will follow. They can be done by everyone. These meditations are particularly helpful in breaking free of fear, negativity, and false attachments and finding true strength and support. As you do these meditations, the attraction to and need for idol worship of any kind will dissolve naturally.

### MEDITATE ON GOD'S GREATNESS

*Know and believe with complete clarity that there is a God who is with you always.* As a way of taking this statement from the realm of belief into direct experience, constantly meditate on all that God gives. As the day goes by, keep becoming aware of the flow of life-giving power that supports and sustains everything. And offer thanks.

### MEDITATE ON GOD'S GOODNESS

*Whatever happens is for good.* Meditate on the fact that God's love and goodness are imprinted in every event, even if you cannot fathom it. Realize that everything which inspires you, everything you love and cherish has its root in God. Find the good in everything that happens.

In Jewish practice meditation includes emotion as well. It is not only the head that must be directed, but the heart as well. Use your meditation on God's goodness to arouse awe of God as well. The awe of God helps you keep the negative mitzvot, to refrain when the time comes to refrain.

CLING TO GOD

*Keep My face always before you.* Ultimately, what is most important is the ability to cling to God, *devekut.* You are to attach yourself to God, be directly aware of the presence of God everywhere, in all people, actions, and events. This is a high level. In order to reach this peak as you meditate, put yourself face-to-face with God. It is said that God's glance gives life, and when you turn your eyes to him, you receive God's glance most fully. The way to do this is to go to a special place where you will not be under the gaze of others and lift your eyes up to God.

It is said that when you turn your face and eyes to God, he will turn his face to you. Keep turning your face, heart, and mind to God in wordless, rapt attention. As you turn all parts of your being to God, you take your attention and longing away from worldly attachments and they dissolve naturally.

## Guidelines to Jewish Practice

WHAT DO YOU PUT YOUR TRUST IN?

Take some time to sit down with yourself and honestly look at what it is you put your trust in.

What or who do you turn to in times of need?

Where you do you spend most time, effort, and money?

Where do you direct your resources?

Now, ask yourself whether you can truly depend on this as a basis for your entire life.

If you wish, write down things that might be serving as idols in your life.

### FINDING TRUE SUPPORT

The first step in finding true support is in letting go of false supports. Although this may be hard to do, it is necessary in order to make room for the true sources of nourishment and support in our lives to make themselves known.

Speak to God daily. Ask for guidance in becoming aware of where your true support is. Stop and listen for an answer. See what happens and what is brought to you in your life.

Take on a mitzvah and practice it daily.

Find an idol in your life and withdraw your energy and devotion from it. Then do it with another. See what happens then.

## Guidelines to
## Zen Practice

### THE SECURITY OF INSECURITY

What are you attached to? What do you feel you cannot do without?

How does this attachment affect your life?

Are you willing to give up one attachment today? See what it's like to be without it? (You can always take it back.)

Tomorrow, give up another.

You will be surprised how good it feels to lose some of them. Others may be harder to let go. Be patient and experiment.

### ESTABLISHING YOUR SENSE OF VALUE

How do you establish your sense of value? What image of yourself are you holding on to?

What can you lose and still be you?

How do you want others to see you?

When you hold on to a false image of yourself and false sense of value, it is natural to accumulate all sorts of things to make yourself feel whole and complete. Let these false adornments go. See who you are then and see where your true support comes from.

Practice zazen daily. Sit as much as you can, as regularly as you can. Regularity is very important. It makes a big difference to sit every day, even if it is only for a few minutes. The consistent practice of zazen affects all your daily actions and guides you in many unexpected ways. And when the time is right, the zazen itself will help you sit a little longer or take any new steps that are appropriate. This can become a huge source of strength, balance, and support in your life.

# CHAPTER 8

# Discovering Yourself: Jewish Identity and Selflessness

*We have been destroying ourselves*
*To adapt to an image, which has been a mirage.*
—ANCIENT ZEN SAYING

W HO AM I? IS a basic Zen koan that is relevant for all of us. Today so many are unclear about who we are, what we want, and where we're going. Identities shift depending on the people we're with, the roles we play, and the changing demands society makes on us. Many define themselves by their accomplishments, relationships, family, or wealth. When these fluctuate or are taken away, they experience an identity crisis, a sense of worthlessness and depression.

*Who am I?* is also a deep question for Jews. Much of Jewish practice revolves around establishing a Jewish identity and living from it. It is considered fundamental for an individual's sense of well-being to discover the truth of his being.

Not knowing who we are, we lean on others and twist ourselves in endless ways to be accepted, to fit in. This hunger for approval and acceptance can easily become a drug. The moment it dissipates, inner suffering, struggle, and self-hatred start all over again. When we function from a false persona, we become jittery and sensitive to every insult and slight. A great deal of suffering comes from living as someone we are not.

What is necessary to feel really good about yourself? Zen practice says that self-hatred arises from living a life of deceit and pretense; but your true nature is always there, waiting for you to return. As Zen students grapple with the question who am I they strip away the masks they live with, learn to let go of artificial roles and games. As they peel these layers off, their original nature makes itself known. A famous Zen saying tells us, when you become you, Zen becomes Zen.

Jewish practice deals with self-hatred differently—through confession, repentance, forgiveness, and living from a character that is worthy of respect. As a result, much Jewish practice focuses on maintaining your identity, not getting lost or assimilating, holding to Torah standards. In keeping with this, there are many mitzvot and guidelines about how to dress, behave, and think. Becoming a real Jew is a lifelong journey.

## Jewish Practice and Identity

Who is a Jew? has many answers, depending on whom you ask. Today there is much debate within the different Jewish denominations about who is and isn't a Jew. These disagreements can reach a fever point, with one group of Jews rejecting another. Much of the upset revolves around different ideas about Jewish practice. In a sense, each denomination is fighting for its understanding of how to relate to Torah.

Orthodox Jews base their entire identity and way of being on Torah and its laws (halacha). Some Orthodox Jews do not want their children mingling or intermarrying with members of other denominations. The exclusion of other Jews is based on a strong wish to maintain the way of life that Torah prescribes. However, the rejection of Jews of different denominations is tricky, as in the process a great deal of animosity can develop. As the Torah forbids animosity toward one another, one who *truly* keeps the Torah must walk a fine line. The battle between the denominations is particularly painful as the heart of Torah keeps telling us that the greatest mitzvah is to love and cherish one another.

Flexible Jews (Conservative, Reform, Reconstructionist, postdenominational) are those who feel it is appropriate to revise the laws and align them with current times and customs. They feel the laws can and must be questioned, updated, and made more relevant to circumstances in this day and age. Flexible Jews revise the services, teachings, and practices, based on their own experiences, tastes, needs, and education.

Then there are secular Jews who may not believe in God but are strongly connected to the Land of Israel and to uplifting and supporting the Jewish people as a nation. Some secular Jews are humanists, philanthropists, scholars, and scientists, living their lives dedicated to the greater good of all. All consider themselves to be Jews and to be living and practicing in a fine way.

As with all koans, the question of who is a Jew must be grappled with by each individual and expressed in his or her life. There is no ultimate answer that fits everybody. The

Wisdom of the Fathers, one of the great Jewish scriptures, answers this question in a simple, inclusive, and straightforward manner, "Who is a Jew? He who praises God continually."

Rather than focus upon issues that divide, it is crucial to focus upon that which unites the Jewish people, their common interests, the ways in which they can contribute to one another. Jews need one another to become whole. This is illustrated by a wonderful story about a dying scholar who felt terrified about facing God. According to the story, his teacher said to him, "Don't worry, when you go to face your Maker, he will not ask you why you did not become Reb Susya, but why you did not become yourself."

## Fostering Jewish Identity

In answer to the question, How do you know a Jew? the Talmud says a Jew maintains his name, his dress, and his language. When you maintain your name, you are reminded of who you are anytime someone addresses you. When you dress as a Jew, you do not blend in. Torah specifically says not to take on the dress, manner, or customs of other cultures you may be living in. This is not because there is anything wrong with the culture but because it is vital to remember who you are. You must always remember why you are here and not lose sight of your purpose. Zen monks and nuns also shave their heads not only to relinquish vanity and delusion, but to be constantly reminded of their purpose in life.

In Torah, women are instructed to dress modestly. Men are instructed to wear specific garments which keep them mindful of the mitzvot they are to perform, and other behavior required from them throughout the day. Both men and women are to retain their original language. This is a way of keeping in touch with the generations, with where you came from and what you are doing here today.

Many people find this offensive, feeling that by separating themselves from others, Jews foster a sense of exclusivity. Unfortunately, this has aroused a great deal of anti-Semitism. However, a Jew is told to maintain his identity not because he is better than others, but because he has a specific purpose, to perform mitzvot, study Torah, and maintain constant awareness of God. He is not here to acquire fortune or fame, but to use all of his time, money, knowledge, and resources to make Torah alive in the world. When he does not perform this function, when he gets involved in other lifestyles, his purpose for being here is lost.

This single purpose has united Jews throughout generations and throughout the different lands and cultures they have lived in. It is easy to get caught up in many enjoyable, beautiful, and worthy lifestyles in different cultures and times. There are many other forms of spiritual service that are also truly meaningful. However, Torah states that Jews are here to engage in Jewish practice. All of the ways in which they are told to separate themselves is for the purpose of not forgetting this. Some accept this, others do not.

### Women Are Women; Men Are Men

In Jewish practice women are women and men are men. One is not superior to the other. Each has equal, though different modes of being, needs, responses, and mitzvot to fulfill. The Lubavitch Rebbe said, "From your father you may learn the things you must do. From your mother you learn who you are." Both are totally necessary. Differences are never blurred but accentuated, so that each can fulfill a unique function. Judaism continually attempts to arrive at harmony through differences. The external aspects of identity reinforce who you are and prevent you from losing your bearings and drifting into empty fantasies.

Although it may seem restrictive to follow such specific directions about how to dress, what name to keep, language to speak, actions to perform, observing them can be greatly liberating. So many individuals these days do not know who they are. They have many thoughts, dreams, and fantasies about who they could be or want to be, but the reality of their life situation is not clear. Others do not see their natural intrinsic beauty. Living without clarity about who we are leads to confusion, wrong choices, and unhappiness. It also causes many people to feel terribly lost.

By accentuating and demarcating identity through dress, language, and name, Jewish practice keeps you reminded of who you are and protects you from wandering off into a world where you do not belong. The negative aspect of this is that you can feel as though you were living out a preset script, without a way to grow or transform. However, Jewish practice does not ask you to stay stuck or dormant. By creating a specific external identity, it offers a *form* through which you can grow. Growth doesn't consist of becoming someone you aren't, dressing differently, or leaving the community and its codes, but working on your inner qualities (*middot*), learning how to live from your essential being, *neshama* (soul). When the external aspects of your life are kept consistent, you are forced to focus on the person within.

But some are unable to live within the framework of the community or identify themselves in normative ways. My father, Henry, heard another call. No matter what the community thought of him, he refused to dress and behave in the expected ways. He was a handsome, smart, successful lawyer, who walked down the street without a yarmulke, wearing a pin-striped suit with a bright tie and the *New York Herald Tribune* folded under his arm. Needless to say, everyone stared. Even though his father was a Torah scholar, many in the neighborhood refused to consider him a Jew.

"Henry," my mother begged, "bend a little. The neighbors are making it hard on us all."

"So, who do you love, Molly? Me or the neighbors? You want me to live a lie? Be proud of me; I'm my own person."

"I am proud," she said, but of course she was not.

"There are a hundred ways to be a Jew, Molly. I'm a good man, I take care of my family, I keep what I want in my heart," he said.

"Your heart's not enough for the neighbors. And now they're even saying that you don't love God."

The very worst thing anyone could say about you, in Borough Park, was that you didn't love God.

"Let them say what they want," he continued, "we're only living here for a little while longer. Soon we're moving out."

"Moving out?" my mother would become frightened. "Where else can we go?"

But no matter how hard he tried to get her out of there, no matter how hard the neighbors made it on her, my mother refused to move off the block or out of the house she was raised in. "Give me one good reason I should move," she would say.

"This place is special. Once you've lived in Borough Park, Brooklyn, every other place is thin air."

## Who Are the Chosen People?

The idea that the Jews are special or the chosen people has caused more difficulty and pain than any other. But it is a case of misunderstanding. It does *not* mean that Jews are better or more beloved by God than others. The Jews were a nation of slaves who were called to take on a mission. What this phrase actually refers to is that Jews are to "choose God." They are the choosing people. A Jew who follows Torah chooses God; when Jews choose to live and practice together, once again, they are making this choice. Any person of any other nation who sincerely wishes to take on the mitzvot and practices of Judaism is most welcome.

True Jewish practice never rejects or looks down on other cultures or nations in any way. When you see this happening, you can be sure the person is not practicing true Torah. In fact, Jewish identity is based around the commandment to "to be a light to all the nations," to serve. Jewish practice focuses on bringing healing, warmth, and light to the entire world.

In keeping with this, a *ger*, a convert to Judaism, is regarded with the highest respect and admiration in Torah. It is said that in the place a *ger* stands, not even a highest sage can stand. We are told to be especially caring, respectful, and welcoming to this person.

## Zen Ways of Knowing Who We Are

In order to help you know yourself deeply and come fully alive, Zen practice does not present a mold to grow into but explores the fundamental question of how we know who we are. It looks at the ways in which we experience ourselves—the ways we know anything at all.

Identity is formed in a complex manner, shaped through the different realms we interact with. In each of these realms, we experience ourselves differently. Much difficulty takes place when these realms become confused. One way we come to know who we are is through social interactions. In the social world we play roles and adopt attitudes that provide a sense of meaning and value. We are then affirmed by the other person's responses to us. A word from another, a glance, or an action can either crush or lift to the heights. We see ourselves through the eyes of others, and in this way we become an object to ourselves.

A second realm is the subjective one, the ways we know and experience ourselves from within. In this realm our inner responses, dreams, images, and meanings give us a sense of who we are. In this realm we are the subject and must answer only to ourselves.

The third realm is the realm of the Absolute, of God or Buddha, our infinite being. When we relate to this realm, we know ourselves as part of the vast universe and are known by the universe simultaneously. In this realm we are subject to eternal laws and must answer to the Absolute—our ultimate destiny.

Conflict arises when we confuse these realms. In the social realm, others see us one way, which may differ from the way we see ourselves. This causes pain and upset. But a social description of who we are describes the effect we have on others. It does not and cannot ever describe our inner being. This is why those who may be revered by others can nevertheless fall into despair. Their inner sense of themselves may differ wildly from the way they are seen through the eyes of others. No matter how much approval they may receive from others, it never fills the void within.

## The Object We Are to Others

It is easy to ascribe more reality to the way others see us than to what we feel from within. When we allow ourselves to be governed by the way others view us, rather than our inner truth, we transform ourselves into a stranger to ourselves. This creates the alienation and loneliness so many feel.

The Zen medicine for this is simple. Choose to be who you are. Validate and live from your inner being, stand planted in the absolute truth of who you are. This is the direction of Zen practice and the essence of all the koans.

Although he didn't know it or refer to it in this way, my father lived his life as a Zen man. He refused to define himself through the eyes of the community but insisted on living from his own sense of himself. And he was nobody's fool either. He gave top advice to his clients, treated each one of them beautifully, and always saw a situation through to the end. Soon after he opened his own law office, more and more people started coming. Not religious people, though. He didn't care. He just put a gold plaque on his door: Myerson & Myerson, Counselor at Law.

"Who's the other Myerson?" Zvi Lichte, a fat guy with a huge belly and a tight black suit stretched over it who lived down the street, taunted him.

"What do you want to know for?" my father said, "You think I'm all alone?"

He was.

"If you're not with God, you're all alone," said Zvi, who was never without his prayer book tucked on him somewhere. "So, you won another case, so what? What kind of law are you practicing anyway? It's not Jewish law."

"There's more in this world than Jewish law," my father proclaimed.

"Says who?" belted out Zvi. "You're becoming like them, Henry. You're melting in the melting pot. They melted in Germany and look what happened to them. Put on a yarmulke, come to shul like you're supposed to. Who are you, better than Moses? It's too easy to forget everything. And your sins, where will they fall? Not on you, maybe, but on your children and your children's children. That's all right with you?"

"Wake up, fellas," my father yelled. "Everyday I get news from Europe on my big radio. We're living in a new generation now."

But in the neighborhood there was no such thing as a new generation. And news from Europe meant nothing either. Only the word of God counted.

After work my father didn't sit on the benches downstairs with others, but went out on the upstairs front porch, to sit under the wide branches of the old cherry tree. Sometimes I went out there to keep him company. "I won't be here forever," he told me over and over. "One day you'll all wake up and I'll be gone. Other places are calling me. Believe me, there are places to go, fabulous places with people who look you right in the eye. I'm packing a bag and putting my new suit in it, the blue one with the big lapels. I'm going tomorrow, and I'm packing tonight."

Everyday I was terrified that he would disappear, but when tomorrow came, nothing was packed.

## Times of Transformation

No matter how we define ourselves, our true being is never stagnant. There is always the longing to go to new places, see people, explore other territories. We change, evolve, mature, develop, sometimes in unexpected, mysterious ways. In the Torah when God was asked who he was, he said—*I am that I am.* This can also be translated also as *I will be that which I will be.* God is never static; there is always his constant presence, along with possibilities and endless change. The same is true in Zen practice; there is the still point within which never moves and the external world which constantly changes. We must stay centered at the still point and simultaneously engage in our tasks in the world of change.

Jewish practice has a different relationship to change and times of transformation. Jewish practice is based on history and life changes. The past is relived in the present and the future is incorporated into each moment of life. The Jewish festivals, among them Rosh Hashanah, Yom Kippur, Sukkot, and Pesach (discussed more fully in Chapter 11), are celebrated during the cycle of seasons throughout the year. They acknowledge and reenact actual events that took place that are to be remembered and reexperienced throughout time. We are to be responsible not only to others but to generations that have passed. Likewise, the future is incorporated into each moment of our lives. Torah teaches that time has an end and the final redemption is eagerly awaited. Each mitzvah we perform brings the individual and the world closer to that moment. History, as we know it, will come to fruition. Great changes will take place in the external world.

Zen practice, on the other hand, is fundamentally concerned with transformation of consciousness, our inner world. From the Zen point of view, only inner transformation will bring the changes we long for in the external world. Zen practice brings us into the eternal present. The past is gone and we are not to carry it around. Repeating the past endlessly only causes our lives to become dormant and static. The future does not exist either. We are constantly practicing this very moment, living on the razor's edge. In Zen practice, the wheel of karma replaces the idea of history moving toward fulfillment. You carry your karma with you and receive the fruits of it endlessly, until through your own efforts, you get off the wheel and awaken. The way you get off the wheel is through practice. New possibilities arise from the freshness of moment, not from a repetition of the past. Only the past arises from the past.

Transformation, or the experience of kensho, or enlightenment, which takes place many times during a life of practice, opens you to the present moment more and more fully. As this happens, you can see that the past is nothing but a dream. It then loses its power to haunt you and grip your life.

In my early days at the zendo, there was a talk by a senior student every Thursday night. Often the talk was given by a gruff guy named Dogo, Don Scanlon, an ex-middleweight boxing champion. I loved listening to him. Not only his talks but who he was inspired me greatly. He had silver hair and a beautiful, old beaten up face. Whenever he talked, the air was filled with expectation.

"I'll be giving the talk for tonight," Dogo said. He didn't smile, didn't have to. He was who he was and nothing else.

"Don't come here and expect to become someone special or something unusual," he continued. "There's nothing unusual about Zen. Maybe it looks like that, but don't be fooled. Come here and expect to work hard. If you're looking for miracles, don't come to Zen. The only miracle in the zendo is that you're here at all. What you end up getting here, is just more of what you are. And sometimes that's not so terrific."

Everyone laughed.

"I've been sitting for about ten years now. And what have I learned? Not much. Just to forget about the past and stay where I am. For years I was beaten up in the ring, but it was nothing compared to what I did to myself. If there's a miracle, it's to learn how to stop beating yourself up—and everyone else. Okay, let's not waste a precious second. This is the time for zazen."

After he spoke, I felt tremendously cheerful, clear, solid, planted in my own life.

No matter what season, life passage, changes, or difficulties life brings, Zen practice stays the same. It does not respond to passing circumstances. You simply return to the zendo, sit down on the cushion, chant the same sutras, and do zazen. You return to your breath and the moment completely and rest in its arms.

## Jewish Practice
## and Life Passages

The movement of time and life passages are especially honored and celebrated in Jewish practice. Not only are they clearly demarcated but are considered to be holy times as well. Ecclesiastes famously teaches, "Everything has an appointed season; there is a time for every matter under the sun. A time to be born and a time to die, a time to plant and a time to uproot what is planted. A time to kill and a time to heal, a time to break and a time to build. A time to weep and a time to laugh, a time to embrace and a time to refrain from embracing. A time to seek and a time to lose, a time to be silent and a time to speak."

During life cycle changes we experience periods of growth and evolution, passages into new forms of being and new aspects of who we are. These life cycle changes are celebrated with ceremonies of many kinds. A new identity is being established. The individual is being ushered into a new phase of being. These rites of passage function on both a psychological and a spiritual level. They ease times of transition and change, call down blessings, put the events of one's life into a larger context, and infuse it with meaning and holiness. They are also great occasions to experience deep fulfillment and thankfulness to God and others. During these celebrations the beauty of life is experienced keenly along with a sense of gratitude for the great gift of being alive.

The most significant times of transition in both Jewish and Zen practice are described below.

### THE BRIS

The eighth day after he is born, a male child is circumcised and officially becomes part of the Jewish nation. This is an extremely powerful ceremony, a holy covenant between the child, God, and the Jewish people. This covenant has to be sealed in the flesh because a Jew always connects to God with both body and spirit. The bris is one of the primary mitzvot.

Many Jews have deep feelings about having a bris as it is the passageway to becoming a Jew for the male child. No matter how little else they practice, when a child is born, this becomes very important to them.

When my first son was born, even though his father was not Jewish, I naturally assumed we would have a bris. To my shock, after he was born and I started to make plans for the bris, my husband refused adamantly. I was out of touch with my family at that time and I couldn't sleep all night, wondering how to handle this. To make matters worse, the following morning, still in the hospital, I heard that the baby wasn't doing well; if things didn't improve, a blood transfusion would be necessary. Deeply shaken, I prayed for help. Finally, it came to me that there was no recourse but to call home, even though some years had gone by. Fortunately my deeply observant brother, Dovid, picked up the phone.

"Help me, please," I said. "A baby's been born, a little boy, and he's sick. I need help to make a bris."

"Of course I'll be there, of course," he replied.

The blood transfusion was scheduled for later that night. My brother quickly arrived at the hospital, and I told him what was going on. He insisted I immediately make a vow to have a kosher bris. Then he ran to pray a late minyan in Borough Park, Brooklyn.

About half an hour after the prayers were said, an hour before the transfusion was scheduled, the baby's blood count turned around. A nurse came rushing downstairs to tell me that the transfusion would not be needed, after all. I gave thanks all night long.

The power of the mitzvah of a bris is enormous. We had a beautiful bris at a friend's apartment, where my brother brought a minyan of Hasids from Borough Park to surround the baby in deep prayer. The reverberation of those prayers have been with my son his entire life and brought him to this day, where he is a committed, practicing Jew.

## BABY NAMINGS

In place of a bris, female children receive Hebrew names at synagogue. When the baby's name is called out, her soul becomes established and joins the Jewish people. Female children do not require a physical procedure because it is said that childbearing and childbirth are the woman's miracle and her deep and abiding connection to God.

## BAR MITZVAH/BAT MITZVAH

At the age of thirteen, male and female children are ready to take responsibility for their own spiritual development and for performing mitzvot. The bar and bat mitzvah is a declaration of this passage. After study in preparation, the child stands before the congregation, reads from the Torah, and gives a talk based on the portion of that week. The purpose of this celebration is to demarcate the beginning of a new chapter in their lives of increased responsibility, observance of mitzvot, and spiritual growth. Unless this is the focus and function of a bar/bat mitzvah, it has nothing to do with Jewish practice.

Traditionally, a bar mitzvah was a simple affair. A young man at the age of thirteen was called up to Torah to receive an honor. It was simply to announce to the community that he was now thirteen, of an age when he became responsible to undertake the mitzvot. A little whiskey was served, some singing. This was not the end of a period of study, but a beginning. This is the point from which true observance, study, and growth was to begin.

Traditionally, young women assumed responsibility for their mitzvot at age twelve. In this regard, an important mitzvah for the young women is modesty and purity. Charity and kindness are also crucial. Unless the true spirit of bar and bat mitzvah are observed, the celebrations can become a distortion of Torah. There are many creative ways to honor this important life cycle which take into account the true meaning of the mitzvah.

### WEDDINGS

Marriage, which I discuss in greater detail in Chapter 10, is a holy event. One of the greatest blessings is to unite in matrimony in order to create a home for God in this world and bring new souls into it. Weddings are occasions of great festivity and celebration. Friends and family come from all corners to rejoice with the couple. The actual preparation for the wedding includes a time of purification. The couple fasts the day before the ceremony and goes to the ritual bath (mikvah) to be cleansed from all impurities and made ready to greet one another in holiness and dedication. Prayers are said when the wedding contract (ketuba) is signed and are said around the bride before the actual ceremony. Kabbalah teaches that when a bride and groom stand under the wedding canopy (chuppah), the souls of their children come to watch and bless them. And, at the time of their wedding and union, heaven and earth are brought closer together; an opening takes place for all prayers to be answered.

After the wedding, the couple does not leave to go to a honeymoon, but remains with family and friends for seven days, during which extra blessings are made upon them. These are called the *sheva bruchas*. Each day during these seven days, there is a party in another family member or friend's home for the couple, and each day the blessings are said. As they participate in the *sheva bruchas,* the couple is not ripped away from family and friends too quickly, rather, family members and friends are brought together and a new, larger family is formed.

## Becoming Jewish:
## Jews by Choice

A *Ger* is a stranger who has come close, a convert to Judaism. The process of choosing to be a Jew—converting—is complicated, as the individual is said to take on a new soul. Traditionally, persons who wished to convert asked three times and were turned away each time before being accepted. The converts agree to take on a life of Torah and mitzvot. This is to make sure they truly want to make this change and realize the full extent of the commitment involved. The actual conversion is the culmination of a long process, through which a new Jewish identity is born. It is not to be taken lightly, as many karmic changes take place.

Over and over it is stated in Torah that a *ger,* a convert or stranger, is to be accorded the highest degree of respect, kindness, and welcome and must be treated with reverence for the difficulty of the commitment he or she has made.

### DEATH AND LOSS

As mentioned, in Orthodox practice, prayers for the dead are said with a minyan twice a day for one year. These prayers not only elevate the soul of the departed, but uplift and ease the mourner's heart as well. When you say these prayers (the kaddish), you feel connected with your loved one and there is still something you can do to help him or her. There is much psychological wisdom embedded in the kaddish. It keeps the relationship alive, with separation coming gradually. Also, when you come to a minyan, you receive support from others. Despite your loss, you are not alone.

The year after a deep loss is a time of healing, transition, and change. During this vital year the kaddish gives you a chance to pause twice a day to remember the departed, be with God, your loved one, and yourself, and digest all that has gone on. You do not forget or suppress what has happened, but enter the experience fully and have an opportunity to integrate the loss into your life.

During the prayers, despite the pain you've gone through, you simply praise God, acknowledging that the world is created according to his will. The kaddish states over and over that life is good. You are constantly directed to see the wonders all around, that everything received is a gift and a blessing. By acknowledging and remembering this, you are enabled to move on when the time is right.

## Ordinary Life
## and Zen Passageways

Zen practice approaches life differently. Ordinary life as it is, is more than enough. This practice, which originally was followed by monks and nuns in monasteries, turned away from life cycles and attachment to family, children, and romantic love. As mentioned previously, the great transformation that Zen practice seeks is awakening. It is considered rare to awaken, and the culmination of many lifetimes of merit and practice. Rather than engage in the conventional life cycles, monks and nuns devoted their entire life energy to awakening and helping others to awaken as well. When enlightenment (or awakening) does take place, there is no special ceremony to acknowledge it. The main ceremonies in Zen practice are connected to different levels of commitment to practice. These are ceremonies which accompany a change of consciousness, dedication, or life direction of the practitioner.

### TAKING THE PRECEPTS (JUKAI)

When an individual accepts the Buddha's precepts, it is called taking Jukai (discussed in Chapter 3 and Chapter 11). Taking the precepts increases commitment and dedication to going forward and is an external manifestation of the level of commitment the student has arrived at on his or her inner journey. Many, though not all, view taking the precepts as a conversion to Buddhism.

### BECOMING ORDAINED

As commitment deepens, some become ordained monks or nuns, who must observe many more precepts. Those who are ordained usually shave their head and publicly dedicate their life to Buddha, dharma, and sangha. (In lay ordinations the head is not shaved.) This is a lifelong commitment not only to practice but to serve others, accepting the role of bodhisattva (one whose life is dedicated to the good of all; discussed below).

### DHARMA TRANSMISSION

Dharma transmission is the public acknowledgment that an individual has not only completed his or her studies but is now a Zen Master, able to guide others. This transmission is rare and is given by the individual's Zen Master. The occasion is marked by ceremonies and great celebration.

## Building Bridges Between Zen and Jewish Expression

At the present time Zen practice is being transposed to the West, where it is being taken on by laymen and laywomen from all backgrounds and streams of thought. Many of these students live in families, work in the marketplace, and are immersed in life cycle changes. Their needs are different from the monks and nuns. In our zendo, along with the practice of zazen, we constantly note and honor life cycles and changes. Blessings are offered at each sitting for anyone who may need them. Other times of special significance and meaning for members of the group are noted and honored as well. We dedicate our sitting to the occasion, chant Hebrew songs or prayers in honor of it (or other prayers or melodies if the individual wishes), read appropriate writings or poetry related to it, and have the individual give a little talk about what it means to him or her. We are now faced with the wonderful opportunity to integrate both practices with our lives as they unfold. Though we may not be taking precepts or becoming ordained, we are new sprouts on branches of very old trees, entwining them both.

## Becoming a Student of Zen

It may take a lifetime to say who is a Jew, but it takes a moment to tell you who is a student of Zen. Fundamentally, if you are breathing, you are a student of Zen. Zen is really nothing special. It is your human life and activity, waking up to reality, discovering what is real beneath all of your beliefs, hopes, and customs—extending warmth and kindness to anyone who comes along.

Students of Zen can be Jewish, Christian, Muslim, atheistic, anything. They can be all ages, races, and nationalities. When Zen is practiced truly, there is no conflict. In fact, Zen puts an end to conflict and alienation, both within the individual and between us all. As you sit and breathe together, it is easy to realize that although you may look, act, or think differently from your neighbor, you are all fingers on one hand. And beautiful in your differences too.

## The True Man of No Rank

The ripened Zen man is called the true man of no rank. It is the person who is left when you take away the ranks, robes, dresses, and decorations of your life. When a true man of rank comes into your life, you immediately recognize him (or her). Your heart is lifted, your burden lighter. It is easier to laugh and to breathe.

In the well-known book by Philip Kapleau, *The Three Pillars of Zen*, the true man of no rank is also called the Zen Fisherman. "The Zen Fisherman is a practitioner who has completed his practice and come down from the mountaintop to return to society, join the world. If you look for him you will not be able to find him. He is roaming about, down at the docks, with the other fisherman. There is nothing special about him either, except that wherever he goes, withered trees start to bloom."

Jewish practice also tells us to work toward becoming humble, nullifying yourself more and more completely to the will of God. This is called *bitul*, or selflessness. You are not here to glorify your personal self but to become a vessel of the divine. Such a person is no different from the Zen true man of no rank. Moses, the greatest Jewish prophet, was said to be chosen because he was the humblest of men. To this day, no one knows where he was buried because we are not to dwell on his greatness but on the greatness of God.

## Guidelines to Jewish Practice

### FOSTERING JEWISH IDENTITY

Spend some time writing down what being Jewish means to you. Is it filled with negative connotations and associations? If so, note it. Become aware. Each of us has the right and responsibility to grapple and find a way to make Jewish identity uplifting and healing, something we can live with.

Who are some of your Jewish role models? Are they positive or negative?

Find or create new role models who are positive and uplifting.

Look into the Torah and find ways in which *you* are called to express your Judaism or your relationship with the Jewish people.

Look and see how you can integrate Jewish practice into your life as you live it now. See how you can make yourself simple and open to the teachings.

If you are not Jewish, explore the seven Noahide laws in the Torah, which apply to all. You will find wonderful connections between Torah and your own religion or practice.

### THE SEVEN NOAHIDE LAWS

According to Judaism, the Noahide laws apply to all humanity. These laws state, "Righteous people of all nations have a share in the world to come." Any non-Jew who lives according

to these laws is regarded as one of the "righteous among gen-
tiles." The Noahide laws are:

- Do not make idols or bow down to them
- Do not murder
- Do not steal
- Do not commit adultery
- Do not blaspheme
- Do not be cruel to animals
- Be just; set up effective laws and courts
  and govern justly

## HONOR YOURSELF AND OTHERS

The Wisdom of the Fathers says, "Who is worthy of honor? He
who honors others." Find ways of honoring yourself and others.
Often we focus on what is worst in ourselves. Instead, focus on
what you do that is worthy of honor. This will increase your
sense of self-worth and enable you to do more that is worthy of
respect. Do the same for others. Notice what is worthy in them
and make a point of acknowledging it. It is so easy to tear others down and so important to do the opposite. The more you
uplift and honor others, the more you honor and uplift yourself.

## Guidelines to Zen Practice

### WHO AM I?

Begin to dwell with this question. Get a journal and write
about it or take the question with you into zazen. Watch
yourself in your daily activities and stop in the midst of your
activities to ask, Who am I? Who is doing that?

When a difficult moment or situation comes to you, stop and feel what is going on and ask yourself, To whom is this coming? Find the one who is having the experience. When you feel insulted or peeved, realize that this reaction is a fleeting part of the false, passing self.

## MAKE FRIENDS WITH ALL OF LIFE

A wonderful way to find out who you are is to make friends with all of life (including yourself). This is based on understanding that what we reject in others is something we cannot accept in ourselves. The more you accept in others, the sooner you will know who you truly are. Extend your warmth, understanding, and sympathy to all you come into contact with.

CHAPTER 9

# Building Relationships: Marriage and Courtship; Monks and Nuns

*Friend, listen, this is what I have to say,*
*The friend I love is inside me.*

—KABIR

TODAY THERE ARE ALL kinds of intimate relationships. In many circles traditional relationships are a thing of the past. Commitment is not automatically a part of anything, including living together or falling in love. Along with these changes, we see increasing divorce, loneliness, and difficulty establishing stable relationships. For many, it has become hard to find a suitable partner and create a lasting home.

Although love and relationships are approached differently in Jewish and Zen practice, the teachings intersect in many ways. Jewish practice insists that we enter all kinds of relationships where love can be expressed. It is in the very process of being in relationship, that we learn what it means to love. Zen practice asks that we first establish the ability to love within.

In the practice of zazen we see and dissolve everything inside ourselves that keeps us from being loving. As we become aware of our fears and constrictions and let them go, we become able to love and care for all. In order to deepen our experience of love, both Jewish and Zen practice reject conventional ideas about what love and relationships are and ask us to adopt a completely new perspective.

## The Jewish Practice of Love

One of the pillars of Jewish practice is the relationship between a man and a woman. This relationship is considered so important that the quality of a person's marriage can tell you everything about who he or she is. A student of Torah wanted to find the best Rebbe to study with. He went around checking on the different ones, asking, "How can I know if this Rebbe is really great?" Finally a well-known scholar answered, "If you want to know the quality of the Rebbe, take a look at how happy he makes his wife."

Jewish practice has a clear-cut view of love and marriage. In American culture, when two people marry we assume they are at the peak of their love. The wedding and honeymoon are thought of as a time of exhilaration, when things are supposed to be perfect. Judaism does not view it this way. In Jewish practice, romantic feelings, which come and go, are not believed to be the foundation for lasting love. Instead, the wedding is just a beginning; the person you marry is there to show you what it means to love. This person is your teacher and will show you the ways you need to grow. Basically, your spouse is your teacher and partner in spiritual growth. When your partner is behaving in a disturbing way, you are to take a step back and realize that she is now simply giving you an opportunity to grow. In your heart you are to thank her for behaving this way; she is teaching you to let go of self-centered focus, to accept differences and not to judge. You are learning patience, humility, and kindness as well.

It is important to focus on caring for and serving your partner, not on how you are being served. In the very deepest sense, your partner is a gift and your relationship is a reflection of your relationship to God. This is an ongoing lesson, and a very central one.

The bond of marriage (*kedushim*), which is discussed above, is considered holy. The marriage ceremony creates holiness around the relationship, blessing and protecting it. When the couple marries, they stand under the chuppah (wedding canopy), which symbolizes protection from destructive influences. The chuppah also symbolizes the new home and shelter being constructed, a new place of love and Godliness.

## The Dangers of
## Falling in Love

Jewish practice teaches that the experience of falling in love is not necessarily healthy; it can be a blessing or a curse. The emotions connected to falling in love can be so intense and create such tumultuous reactions that unless you are prepared, they can cause difficulty and blindness of all kinds. For example, you may not know if what you feel is love or some kind of fantasy infatuation, similar to being intoxicated. When the intoxication fades, you sober up and can see things clearly. Likewise, when you come down from a fantasy infatuation, you may wonder what you ever saw in the person in the first place.

In the Bible it is said that when Rebecca first saw Isaac, she experienced such intense emotions love that she nearly fell off her camel. However, because she had so completely bound herself to him beforehand, even before they were introduced, she was able to recognize him as her soul mate. Her reaction came from recognizing and remembering events that occurred outside time and space.

Another biblical example of love at first sight is Jacob and Rachel. Jacob immediately knew he was going to marry Rachel. His love at first sight was so intense that it enabled him to single-handedly roll back the boulder covering the well. And he cried, for he sensed he would not merit being buried with her. He also sensed the existence of difficulties and delay before they cold be married. In both cases, the individuals were prepared to meet their soul mates, so events proceeded as planned. Psychological and spiritual preparation for an event serves as a protective shield which controls and directs the intense emotions of the heart.

## Soul Mates:
## The Yearning for the Partner

The sages say that the divine image includes both a male and a female aspect. A single individual is only "half a body" and that "it is the way of man to search for woman." According to Jewish teaching a truly matched couple are two parts of the same soul. For this reason the two are destined before birth to unite in matrimony. When you are therefore longing for your true partner, you are longing for the other part of your soul. Spiritually speaking, ultimately, you are longing to be united with God.

Longing creates the tension that draws male and female together. Man seeks woman and woman yearns for man. Sexual attraction is driven by your search for your divine image, your desire to become whole. The ultimate union of male and female energies is a theme that runs through the entire process of creation. In keeping with this, a marriage between two human beings is an analog of the marriage of divine forces. In marriage, man and woman regain their original state as they become one.

Everyone wants to find a soul mate. Although it is considered a very great blessing and privilege to find this person, all may not be ready for it. Jewish practice teaches that there may be growth or repair that must take place before you are ready for this encounter. You may first have to develop to a level where you can attract and be suitable for the person who is meant for you. If you want to find your soul mate, first attend to your soul; nourish it and prepare for this encounter by refining your character and increasing your goodness. Then you are to pray. Be aware of what you are praying for. Do not ask for a trophy wife, a millionaire, or a fantasy come true. Ask for a partner who will reflect the best in you. The sages teach that "a good wife" is one who makes her husband conscious of the depths of his own will to be good.

## How Do We Know It's the Right One?

An eternal question that haunts many is how will you know if you've found the right partner? Is it love at first sight, or infatuation? Is chemistry necessary? s the presence of If there's a strong, mutual attraction are you to ignore it? Is it a sign?

Doesn't a strong attraction mean that there is something each partner has to give, receive, or learn from the other? What happens when the person is from a different religion, race, or lifestyle?

Many stay in relationships for years, all the time maintaining that they are not with the right person. Others, even while dating, can never settle down. They always feel the right one is just around the corner. No person they actually meet, however, can live up to their dream. Others mistake feelings of attraction and chemistry with love. When feelings of attraction die down, they are sure that love is gone. Others equate feelings of dependency and attachment with being in love. They feel that if they cannot exist without the other person, then surely this is love.

Jewish teachings state that it is harder for God to bring a man and woman together than it was for Him to split the Red Sea. The long-standing Jewish practice of arranged marriage reflects this difficulty. These couples are brought together by their families and communities. The introductions are based on mutual life style, goals, values, and spirituality. Both parties are well-known to their family and friends. No one is forced to marry. Introductions arranged in this tasteful manner spare both parties embarrassment and allow them to avoid wasting time and emotion on matches that would not fulfill their highest good.

Arranged marriages seek to avoid the confusion we find in many relationships and protect the couple from the heartache many endure in finding and living with their life partners. From both Jewish and Zen points of view, confusion and suffering in relationships comes simply from a lack of understanding of what love truly is and how to help it grow.

## The Zen Practice of Love

Zen practice steps back from the chase and quietly asks what are we truly seeking and what is it we lack. Many who crave a relationship feel that something is missing; they have lost a precious treasure and are now searching for it everywhere. It must be their soul mate, who may be nowhere to be found. If they cannot or do not find their perfect partner, they are unworthy or have failed.

But who is searching, and who must be found? From the Zen point of view, this search for ourselves in another person is dangerous and misleading. Just as you are, you are complete and whole. Nothing need be added. Your original nature encompasses all; it is neither male nor female, big nor small. The feeling that you lack something comes from your obsession with seeking your good outside of yourself.

As mentioned above, traditionally, Zen practice took place among monks and nuns in monasteries. Monks and nuns were called "those who left home seeking the way." They renounced household duties, responsibilities, and relationships such as marriage, family, possessions, money, and sex in order to find enlightenment. These individuals would train for years at monasteries with different masters. Some would then leave and practice alone. Others would establish small temples. Zazen practice was for the priesthood. Although their ultimate enlightenment was brought back into the world and shared with others, their training and lives were lived apart. Attaining and maintaining enlightenment in the midst of a busy, crowded, confusing, greedy world was considered much more difficult. It was also believed that the life of a householder, a married person with children, with social and financial obligations, would keep an individual mired in samsara (the cycle of birth and death), governed by desire and karma.

Today, Zen practice has been transplanted to the West where it is largely practiced among people who are referred to as householders. These practitioners have the wonderful opportunity of both doing zazen and integrating their practice with the marketplace of life. Ultimately, a practice such as this cannot be shaken, no matter what storm appears. Practitioners have husbands, wives, friends, and business associates who become part of their training and part of the way.

## Seeking the Way

Zen students may not seek soul mates, but they do seek "the way." Rinzai, a patriarch of Zen, says, "One person has left home but is not on the way. The other has not left home but is ever on the way." Actually, this is a koan. It is asking, Where is the way, what does it mean to be on it? And what does it mean to leave home? Is it even possible?

True Zen students are on the way with every step they take, when with others and when alone. They are on the way whether living in a monastery or with a family, working at a job or dealing with financial pressures. Indeed, they can leave home and be on the way right in the middle of a full life, caring for family, loving their partner, earning a living. Where is this way they are on?

Leaving home and being on the way means renouncing craving, possessiveness, attachment. No matter where you are living, in a monastery or a family, it is easy to cling to those you are close to, place many demands and expectations on them, create obligation, guilt, debt, and remorse. You leave home when you release this attachment, when you give up the demand that others treat you a certain way. You leave home while living in the family when you let go of the idea that it's up to your family or friends to give your life meaning or make you happy. When you do that, you can be a householder, stay with your family, and be on the way as well.

Some who leave home have a partner and some do not. Either way is fine. When practice deepens, ultimately you will not feel lonely without a partner. On the other hand, you will also be able to be in a relationship and not feel trapped with someone at your side. Instead, you will be connected to all people you meet, able to be with them fully when they're here, and when it's time for them to go, let them fully depart.

When you leave home and enter the way, you not only feel concern for the members of your group but you become part of the human family, able to extend compassion and concern to all. You realize that the whole world is your family, and every place is the right place to be. As Soen Roshi said, "Wherever I go, is my home in eternity." The way is endless and all pervasive. You enter the way within.

## The Jewish Practice of Marriage

In Judaism, the way is found at home. The place to find God, or spiritual fulfillment, is never away on a mountaintop but at home, at the kitchen table. The table is the altar; the food and the prayers are the offerings. The highest joy and blessing is to create a home, which becomes a vehicle of holiness, warmth, hospitality, and wisdom, where all are welcomed.

Each relationship is significant, but of all relationships, marriage is considered the most intimate and able to bring the blessings, warmth, and support you need. Due to the protection of your marriage vows, you can feel safe enough to be full open with your partner, keep nothing from him. In marriage all is intensified, both the good and difficult times. These challenges are to be expected, faced, and dealt with. Without them, you could not truly become all you are meant to be. Not only are you to marry, but to raise a family as well.

In Jewish practice, not only love but sexual fulfillment is considered crucial. It is important to keep sexual desire alive, to feel deeply wanted and cared for. A couple that experiences physical as well as emotional fulfillment can provide the warmth and nurturing needed by children. Difficulties in the family are more likely to occur when the love and intimacy between the husband and wife are not satisfying.

## The Role of a Wife

The wife has many spiritual and physical functions. One is to guard and defend her husband. In addition, she has the power to make her husband righteous; with her help he can stand against the forces of difficulty that challenge him all the time. A man is told to listen to his wife and learn from her.

A good wife is considered a great blessing. It is said that a wife is the source of her husband's sustenance, and that blessing comes to a man's household for the sake of his wife. Beyond that, in order to create a home, which is a receptacle for the holy spirit (*shechinah*), a wife is essential.

## The Role of a Husband

In Jewish practice, there are three specific duties a husband must fulfill. He must give his wife physical pleasure, provide her food, and buy her clothes. Beyond this he must honor and cherish her and know that she is his deepest connection to God. The Torah states, "One should eat and drink less than his means allow, dress in accordance with his means, and honor his wife and children beyond his means."

A husband is to supply his wife with strength, protection, love, and connection to God. In observant communities, it is considered a great honor for a woman to have a husband who is learned in Torah. One main criterion in choosing a husband is not how rich he is or what kind of job he has, but how learned he is. Many wives work to support their husbands so that they can devote their time to studying Torah.

Rabbi Akiva, one of the greatest sages in all of Torah, who was involved with bringing forth Kabbalah, was a simple man who for many years knew nothing of Judaism. He fell deeply in love with the daughter of a strict Rabbi, who was at first horrified by the match. However, the daughter also fell in love with him. They married and Rabbi Akiva wanted to study Torah. He was forty at the time.

His wife sent him away to pursue his studies. She was thrilled that he wanted to do so and worked for years to support him. After fourteen years he came back, surrounded by many disciples, but realized he needed more time. His wife gladly sent him off for another fourteen years and continued working.

When he returned fourteen years later, among the many people who rushed to greet him was his wife. One of his disciples saw a woman running to him, getting too close, and tried to keep her away. Although she looked different after all these years, Rabbi Akiva recognized her immediately and said, "Let her come. For without her work, your Torah and my Torah would not exist."

This story shows the different forms marriage can take and how crucial a woman is to her husband's spiritual development. Ultimately his spiritual development becomes a blessing for her as well. Marriages are spiritual partnerships, and each couple serves in the way given to them.

## The Bitter and the Sweet

In these days when there is prolonged trouble in a relationship, when anger and upset continue, couples resort to blame, separation, and divorce. Individuals say, "At first things were fantastic; we were thrilled with each other all the time. Now there's nothing but heartache and complaints. We try to talk it over, but it doesn't work. Where did the love go?"

Of course the love didn't go anywhere. Love is always present and available to those who know what love is and how to make it grow. Both Zen and Jewish practice teach that love has nothing to do with emotion but is always based on right action, right speech, and right state of mind. In Zen practice, zazen puts the person on a firm footing, not depending on another, but at home with himself and therefore fully able to be with another. From the Jewish point of view, all the mitzvot are basically deeds of love.

Some of the greatest Rebbes had wives who treated them harshly. They accepted this difficulty with the greatest of grace, understanding that whatever bitterness they were receiving was a way for them to grow; it was both a cleansing and repair of their souls. It was also a way for them to learn how to extend kindness in return. What made them great Rebbes was that they were able to take their Torah learning and live it out with their wives (no small task). The relationship between men and women is complicated; it is intended to be so. Neither party can leave the relationship; each must turn to the other to have his or her needs met and thus both are forced to learn to overcome negative emotions and selfishness, to extend themselves and learn how to really love. The book of Proverbs states, "He who has found a woman has found good." Yet Ecclesiastes says, "And I find woman more bitter than death." The experience of being in such an intimate relationship is always both bitter and sweet. This intimate, intense relationship comes to teach the partners how to deal with both. When you try to control your partner, are driven by ego, or have the person there simply to serve your needs, the relationship turns very bitter. Your task is to learn how to take bitterness and make it sweet, to learn the true purpose of relationships, how to make love grow.

## Zen and the Practice of Relationship

On the deepest level, there is no difference between Jewish and Zen teachings in relationships. Because Zen practice is founded on oneness, ultimately, as we sit, the experience of struggle with and separation from others diminishes. Instead, we grow to see each person as another part of ourselves. A relationship becomes like looking in the mirror;

whatever we cannot accept in another is simply something we are rejecting in ourselves. The person we're having trouble with has come into our life to help us see and accept this aspect of ourselves. As we accept others, whoever they may be, our sense of oneness broadens and we learn what love really means.

In Zen, as in Judaism, relationships come to teach us to grow. We do not relate to another person as an object to fulfill our cravings or needs. We do not use another to inflate our ego in any way. Each person we are in relationship with is to be served and honored. Joko Beck, a wonderful modern-day Zen teacher, says, when you meet someone, say in your mind, "How may I serve you?" This establishes the tone of the relationship. When a relationship that was sweet becomes bitter, realize that this due to karma that has ripened. It is a chance for you to grow.

Hakuin was a great monk who lived simply in a hut in a little village where he was admired by all. The villagers praised him daily and brought food and other offerings. One day a young woman in the village became pregnant, and the father of the child left town. Frightened, the young woman told everyone that Hakuin was the father of her child. The horrified villagers immediately began blaming him and refused to bring offerings or food. When Hakuin heard the news, he simply said, "Is that so?"

The child was born and the young woman gave him to Hakuin to raise. Hakuin accepted the child with open arms, simply saying, "Is that so?" He raised the child lovingly for a number of years, when suddenly the father of the child returned to the village. Ashamed of what had happened, the young man returned to claim the child and care for him and the child's mother.

The couple told the villagers what had happened, and the blame Hakuin had received now turned to praise once again. Hakuin simply said, "Is that so?" The couple also came to reclaim their child. Hakuin gave him back to his parents lovingly, once more saying, "Is that so."

This story describes the essence of Zen practice with relationships. Whatever came to Hakuin he accepted lovingly, simply noticing what was going on. When it was time to care for the child, he did so with open arms. When it was time to give the child back, he did so as well. Praise and blame were the same to Hakuin. He was not dependent on the views of others but was connected to his true self, fully aware of his function in the world. When something came to him, he welcomed it; when it was time for it to leave, he let it go. He was able to love without attachment and was free from being tossed about by praise and blame.

## The Jewish Practice of Growing in Love

In Jewish practice, without the presence of God in a relationship, it is very difficult to deal with hard times. The Torah says, "There are three partners in every marriage: the man, the woman, and God." The way to bring God into a marriage is to practice the mitzvot related to marriage. These mitzvot become the foundation on which the marriage is built. When they are followed, the relationship becomes healthy and strong and you have the tools to deal with difficult times. Some of these mitzvot follow.

## DO NOT CONCEAL
## ANYTHING FROM EACH OTHER

"Do not hide away or conceal anything from each other. Live together in love and affection." A husband and wife are to be a place for one another where all can be open, trusted, and revealed. Honest, open, ongoing communication is the heart of a marriage and a great mitzvah. Deceit, lies, withdrawal, and other forms of dissembling are forbidden. This is considered a precious relationship and its core is based on truth.

## GUARD YOUR VOWS CAREFULLY

Wedding vows are to be carefully guarded. They regulate the man's relationship not only with his wife, but with other women as well. This protects the relationship and also protects the man from being seduced. In Orthodox communities, a man is not permitted to be alone with another woman. At gatherings men and women sit at separate tables. There are many reasons for this. First, when men and women sit separately, men do not have an opportunity to become too familiar with or attracted to other women. This protects the wife's feelings and decreases competition among women for men's attention. This allows the women to be closer to one another and have a stronger experience of sisterhood and female bonding. The same is true of men. Women dance with women at celebrations and men dance with men.

## LEARN TO UTILIZE TENSION POSITIVELY

Rather than deny the fact that tension between a husband and wife seems to be inherent, Jewish practice structures the marital relationship so that this tension will be channeled constructively. Rabbi Manis Friedman says that tension is inevitable because the male is fundamentally different from female, physically, emotionally, mentally. The couple once were strangers and on some level will always remain strangers.

In order to be in harmony, certain fundamental resistances between the sexes must be overcome. A man has to overcome his resistance to commitment, and a woman has to overcome her resistance to invasion. The love between a husband and wife will have to overcome these differences, again and again. Because of this, their love is not calm or consistent, nor should it be. It needs fuel, sparks, and energy to bridge the differences. Rabbi Manis Friedman calls this the energy of fiery love.

Fiery love creates a continual experience of distance, separation, and then coming back together again. When the two are distant, the desire to merge is intensified. If a couple becomes too familiar or comfortable, their love will not flourish, as the fire is absent. This fiery sexual love is created by constant withdrawal and reunion. Fighting in a marriage creates this distance, so the husband and wife can then feel their longing for one another and reunite. Rather than resorting to fights or anger, however, the Torah provides a positive solution to this built-in need to come together and to be apart—the laws of family purity.

### TAKE TIME TOGETHER AND TIME APART

The mitzvah of family purity says that the couple should refrain from sexual relations during the wife's menses and a week after that. During that time there is no touching, sitting close by, or sleeping in the same bed. This creates an enforced but positive separation between them. They are being forced to take needed time apart and given an opportunity to have their own separate space. This protects the intimate, romantic aspect of marriage, which thrives on withdrawal and reunion. It keeps the relationship exciting and fresh.

Time together and time apart also protects the woman from feeling like an object to be used and protects the man from having to constantly perform, constantly be in relationship. It honors the fact that in an optimal relationship there must be time for each individual to be separate, to have time together and time apart.

## Domestic and Spiritual Abuse

Unfortunately, today we are aware of a great deal of domestic abuse. Particularly in the area of relationships, it is easy to use spiritual teachings to cover up abuse, or to use the teachings to hurt, blame, or judge one another. Due to the intimacy of the relationship, some marriage partners feel they have a right to control, judge, or misuse their spouse. Some use spiritual laws to refuse to give their wives a proper divorce (*get*) when one is appropriate. These men keep these wives, who are called agunot, chained in a no-man's-land, unable to remarry and go on with their lives. This is not spiritual practice but spiritual abuse, using the teachings in a distorted manner to harm another. True spiritual practice always guards the freedom and integrity of both individuals. When freedom, love, respect, equality, mutuality, and integrity are not present, it is not a Torah relationship, no matter how it may appear externally.

There are also other ways in which the teachings can be distorted and turned into a form of abuse. In some communities, there is undue pressure to marry. When an individual does not or cannot marry, is gay, or marries someone who is not approved of, perhaps someone of another religion, the consequences can be severe. Under the guise of the teachings, individuals are then cast aside, rejected, punished, humiliated, and made to feel worthless. Once again, in my view, this has nothing to do with true spiritual practice, but is blatant aggression and another form of spiritual abuse.

When an individual is not acceptable unless she marries the right person, when her boundaries are violated or private life is probed by those in the community, this is not Torah; it is spiritual abuse. Spiritual abuse has driven many individuals away from temples and practice and has crushed many who have remained. The best antidote for it is to open your eyes to the true teachings, which are always based on love, and not to give authority over yourself to anyone. You always have intrinsic value, and anything which attempts to take that away is not spirituality but abuse and control.

Like Hakuin, described above, when difficult moments come, look clearly at what is going on and say, Is that so? It is also helpful to remember the teaching of Buddha which puts things in their proper place: "Before you try to straighten another, do a harder thing. Straighten yourself."

Constructive guidance always comes from a person who has straightened himself. A true friend, congregant, or teacher cares about what is beneficial for you. He is not there to crush but to lift you. The same is true for practice itself. If there are some mitzvot you cannot do, there are many others waiting. Some excel in one mitzvah, some in another. This is as it should be. To be condemned for not doing certain mitzvot is nothing more than spiritual abuse. Some of us can marry, have families, and live happily in community. Others hear a different call.

## Zen and the
## Practice of Being Alone

A majority of people in the world live as couples, walking two by two. It is natural to want a partner and to feel as though you belong. And yet beneath this need to be in relationship often lies a great fear of being abandoned, being ostracized, or being alone.

But some hear a different call; their way is made as they walk along. They relinquish their fear of standing on their own. They do not live for the praise of others, or to deflect rejection or blame. This does not mean that they do not love, just the opposite. When we stay in relationship out of fear of being alone, this is not love. We are simply using the person to allay our fear. As we give up dependence on others, we grow to see that we can never be abandoned; we are always with the One.

## Becoming Intimate
## with All of Life

Like love and relationships, Zen is built on paradox. What seems to be one thing turns into another. What we hope and yearn for loses its taste. What we believe to be true is revealed as illusion. The love we initially feel turns into disappointment; disappointment turns into hurt; hurt turns into forgiveness; forgiveness turns into love once again. The couple retreats to separate corners; the one who walks alone is never lonely. The wheel keeps turning.

Through practice, we become intimate with all of life. This intimacy is not necessarily romantic or sexual in nature (though it can be). To begin, we become intimate with our own experience; the way is right under our feet. As we become accepting of all experience, we do not have to erect walls to shut anything out. Then we are naturally present to the never ending panorama life offers; intimate with the sunset, trees, oceans, animals, seeing there is nothing to reject.

When we do not choose one person over another, reject or label anyone good or bad, we finally become able to hold the entire world in the palm of our hand. When we can accept all beings exactly as they are, this is what it means to love. It is a vast love, encompassing all that life brings.

## Guidelines to Relationship Practice

### COMMITMENT AND INTIMACY: HOW LOVE GROWS

Both Zen and Jewish practices show how to approach relationships as spiritual practice. Before undertaking either of them, however, it is necessary to become aware of how you are in relationships now; the reality of your life as it is today. Then the next steps can be taken.

### GENERAL OVERVIEW OF PRESENT RELATIONSHIPS

Spend some time answering the following questions in a journal:

> What does a relationship mean to you? How do you build a lasting relationship?

> What does it mean to you to be committed?

What are several ways in which you feel able to be committed? What are several ways you avoid commitment?

To whom have you given your word? Can you be depended on?

What is the relationship between intimacy and commitment in your mind? Is true intimacy possible without commitment? Think this over, write it down.

## PRACTICING COMMITMENT AND INTIMACY

Look at what you feel you would have to do to be committed in a relationship.

Take one item from the list and actually do it today. Tomorrow do something else.

If you've let your word slip, fix it. Renew some commitment that may have lapsed.

Look at what intimacy means to you in a relationship.

Do something that represents intimacy today. Tomorrow do something else.

Tell someone close to you what she means to you. Write a thank-you note that is overdue. Ask for something you may need or want. Do it without making a demand.

Keep a record of what you do and the reaction it produces. Do this for a week.

Now go back to your list and add new items to it. Expand your practice of both commitment and intimacy and see how they intertwine.

These exercises build emotional muscles and strength. As you practice them, your ability to grow in relationships will expand exponentially.

## Guidelines to Jewish
## Practices in Relationships

The Torah establishes an ideal of human interaction and relationship, something to work toward. Relationships are a way to arrive at self-nullification and become closer to God. For some individuals this form of relationship (or marriage) is attainable. For others, it is not. We see many today who cannot or do not wish to practice in this way. And some who may want this cannot find an appropriate partner to share this lifestyle with.

If this is your situation, it does not mean that you cannot live a life based on Torah and attain happiness and fulfillment. Unfortunately, many have turned away from Jewish practice because they feel that unless they fit into a normative mode they are unacceptable or lost. This is not true. Apply the Torah teachings in any way you can, to any relationship you are presently in. The teachings are not meant to create outcasts but to bring harmony and love to all.

If you are in a marriage or other relationship and care to apply some of the mitzvot relating to marriage to your relationship, here are some you can start with (any others mentioned above can be applied as well).

Begin by viewing your wife, husband, or partner as your spiritual teacher.

No matter what your partner says or does, see this as an opportunity for you to grow. In your mind thank your partner for the challenge they are presenting to you.

Understand that tension in a relationship is natural. Make sure that each of you have time together and time apart. No one can give continuously. Your partner is a precious gift to you, a way to become closer not only to them, but to God and to your soul.

Spend time in prayer with your partner. Ask God to come into your lives and guide your relationship.

Give thanks for the wonderful parts of the relationship, all that both of you constantly give and receive.

Dedicate your relationship to welcoming and serving others. Open your home to guests; share beautiful meals with them. Be a source of light and love.

## Guidelines to Zen Practice in Relationships

Zen practice asks that we learn to love without attachment, become able to give and be present, while at the same time granting the other autonomy and space. There is a huge difference between being close to someone and grasping or clinging to that person. We all have tasted both. We must learn to let go of controlling and turning people into objects to fulfill our needs.

Whatever relationship you are in, just be with the other person, without expecting or demanding anything.

Allow the relationship and person to be exactly as it is.

Ask (whether out loud or in your own mind), "How may I serve you?" This puts the relationship into another frame of reference. Remember, you are not here to dominate or impress, but to make an offering of yourself.

Bow to the person in your mind, before and after an interaction. Salute the beauty within him or her. As you do this, you bring the beauty forth.

## Letting Others Be Who They Are

Make a list of all the demands you place on others, and on yourself, to be a certain way.

Make a list of that which you cling to in relationships, what you feel you couldn't get along without.

As you begin the practice of letting go, you may feel uneasy. But as you continue, these feelings will subside and will be replaced by the taste of a new kind of love.

Day by day, let go of one thing that you cling to, including a person. Let go of your attachment to him or her. Stop trying to change, control, and cling to that person. Let everything be as it is between you. See what happens as you do.

As this practice progresses, you will notice that you are experiencing more enjoyment and well-being in relationships and also making room for new people to be attracted to you as well.

Expand the list of what you are attached to and what you can let go of now.

Expand the list of individuals you are willing to offer the space to be who they are.

Practice this on a daily basis.

See your life burst into bloom.

CHAPTER 10

# Making Peace in the Family and the World: Forgiveness and Renunciation

*Heaven is not just somewhere you go.*
*It is something you carry with you.*
—LUBAVITCH REBBE

IN JEWISH PRACTICE THE family is the core on which the world is built. It is the place where we are taught to share, love, and grow into the person we are meant to be. It is a place to return for comfort, validation, and support. The family is also a place where we are challenged and confronted with intense, often conflicted emotional relationships. Family members are the ones who have meant the most to us, those to whom we have turned to fill our deepest needs and desires, are also the ones to whom we are most vulnerable. In order for us to have good relationships in other areas of life, it is crucial to learn how to be at peace with our family. This is probably the most difficult challenge of all.

In Zen practice the students with whom we practice are called the sangha (discussed more fully below). In this spiritual family, we also experience and work through our deepest needs and vulnerabilities. Through years of practicing together a level of intimacy between sangha members develops that may be deeper than many members of a biological family. Sangha members offer unconditional acceptance, encouragement, and sanctuary to one another. As Soen Roshi once said, "Among the sangha, harmony is most important."

In Jewish practice, the home is the sanctuary. However, a home cannot be a sanctuary unless there is peace in the family that lives there. Making peace is a great mitzvah, and peace in the family is uppermost. This is called shalom bais. From the point of view of Jewish practice, difficult family relationships are not a matter of chance. Family members are given to one another as teachers, or for a tikkun (explained in Chapter 6), to correct past deeds and errors. They are also a means of overcoming difficulties or developing new parts of yourself. Whether or not you like a family member, the bond goes deep. When one of you is in trouble, the others feel it. Overlooking the difficulties and needs of your brothers or sisters is considered a sin. The way you treat your brothers and sisters is a training ground for your relationship with people in the world at large. The same is true for sangha members.

Ultimately, the way you relate to your original family is the way you will relate to others as well. It is easy to project unfinished business with your family onto other individuals in your life, or turn to them to provide the warmth and caring you were deprived of at home. This is a mistake, as no person in the present can make up for the loss or pain you suffered long ago. When you learn to heal the pain of your childhood, then all other relationships can flourish and grow.

Judaism teaches that when family life is not stable and honored, the very roots of what is means to be human are called into question. Today we see great changes in family structure. Family members live far from one another or have very little contact, family traditions are losing their force, an increasing number of interreligious and interracial marriages are taking place. These situations present new kinds of challenges, and we need new ways of understanding and relating to them.

## The Jewish
## Practice of Family

When the family is run according to the laws of Torah, peace is created naturally, differences are easily healed, and the family becomes a sanctuary. There are many mitzvot which describe how to do this. Peace must be made and kept on a daily basis. Although some of these mitzvot also apply to the world at large, the place where they must be originally taught and practiced is the family. Learning and practicing these mitzvot is the real gift parents can offer their children, the real protection against future difficulty.

Some fundamental mitzvot of making peace in the family and in the world follow. Although a couple of these mitzvot were discussed in Chapter 3, they are elaborated below because they are so fundamental in the process of making peace in relationships. All the other mitzvot included below describe different dimensions of making peace or practicing kindness. Although different mitzvot may seem similar to each other, if you look carefully, you will see that each one addresses a different aspect of the need for kindness and points to different circumstances where it must be practiced.

## YOU ARE
## YOUR BROTHER'S KEEPER

No matter what differences exist, no matter what disappointment, hurt, rivalry, or resentment, overcome this and put your brother's and sister's needs above your own. Deeds of kindness are needed, no matter how you feel. You are to share, listen, go out of your way, put your selfishness aside. You are your brother's and sister's keeper. Take good care of them.

## LOVE YOUR NEIGHBOR
## AS YOURSELF

This foundational mitzvah is discussed in Chapter 3. Your neighbor is anyone and everyone who is beside you; a brother or sister, a friend, an acquaintance, and even a so-called enemy. How can you love God truly if you do not love, care for, and cherish the family and neighbors God gave you? When you practice this mitzvah, an individual or a family member you may think of as an enemy one day, can turn into a friend the next. Nothing is set in stone. If you see someone as an enemy, you call forth the darkness within her; when you view her through the eyes of love, you call forth the best in her. Practicing this mitzvah wholeheartedly creates miracles. Additionally, the mitzvah says to love your neighbor as you love yourself. You must therefore also love yourself, honor and acknowledge the best within. Remember, in Judaism, love is always a verb, based on appropriate actions, both toward yourself and others.

## HAVE MERCY
## ON YOUR FRIEND

The mitzvah to have mercy on your friend is another way of loving him. You are to have as much mercy on your friend, his money, and his honor as you would on your own. If he is being dishonored, protect him. If his money or other resources are at risk, help him take good care of them. Be mindful of all aspects of your friend's life. This does not mean being intrusive but being conscious of what's going on in your friend's world and always willing to extend a helping hand.

## UNLOAD THE BURDEN
## FROM THE DONKEY

"If you see the donkey of someone whom you hate lying under its burden, you shall surely help with him. It is your duty to unload it." Torah teaches that whether or not you like or dislike a person who has a donkey (or any other animal) that is stumbling, you must stop and help. Don't pass by any person or animal that is loaded down with burdens and not extend yourself. If the donkey falls or stumbles again, load and unload it, even a hundred times. This teaches us not to offer help in a token manner, but to do everything thoroughly, to the very end. We see this same teaching in Zen practice, which tells us to sit deeply, pay attention to every little detail of our life, and offer ourselves wholeheartedly to everything we do.

This mitzvah is a prototype of how to make peace both in the family and in the world. Everything that needs help is responded to; a person, his family, friends, animals, or anything belonging to him. Whenever you see a need, step in and help unconditionally.

### RETURN A LOST OBJECT TO THE OWNER

All objects and possessions are part of a person's soul. You are to return everything that is lost to its proper place and rightful owner. This can refer to more than physical objects. See if you can return a person's lost self-esteem, or his joy in life.

### MAKE A FENCE FOR YOUR ROOF AND
### REMOVE ALL OBSTACLES FROM YOUR HOUSE

Another way of loving your neighbor is to protect her from harm. You must be careful to protect all who come into your space, not to create any danger or leave anything unattended that might cause harm. Nothing you do, say, or have should become a snare or a stumbling block to your fellow man.

### JUDGE EVERYONE FAVORABLY

This crucial mitzvah for creating peace in the family, in the world, and within yourself is also discussed in Chapter 3. At all times you are to judge everyone favorably, including yourself. For example, when something occurs which could cause conflict or upset, find a positive explanation for it. Do not allow negative expectations or fears to take over. Instead, focus on the positive aspects of the person and relationship. Think of all the positive explanations you can for this situation. This prevents you from indulging in negative interpretations of what's going on, prevents trouble from escalating, and puts you at peace.

### DO NOT RESPOND TO AN INSULT

Insults are common in families and everywhere else. When someone insults you, remain absolutely silent; never respond in kind. The insult is a test. When you can be silent and respond humbly, you transform the insult into a gift. The Torah teaches that if you do not give in to your impulse and respond negatively, the insult clears you of past wrongdoing and you then receive more light and strength. Some Rabbis of old would wait eagerly for insults, be thrilled when they received one, so they would have a chance to respond humbly and have their sins cleared away.

This teaching is also emphasized in Zen practice, and beautifully articulated by a sage of old Shantideva: "When someone hurts me, may I regard him as a great sacred friend." That person is a friend because he has come to help clear your karma, balance your wrongdoings, and teach you how to forgive.

## WATCH WHAT YOU SAY
## AND DO WHAT YOU PROMISE

Integrity is crucial. Always keep your word. When you give your word, you raise the hopes, dreams, and expectations of others. Breaking your promise causes pain. The entire structure of human relations is based on your ability to be counted on and trusted, to keep your word.

## FORGIVE ONE ANOTHER

Forgiveness is such a huge topic and mitzvah in Judaism and in the practice of making peace, that an entire holiday, Yom Kippur, the Day of Atonement, is devoted to it. In preparation for Yom Kippur, you are to call each person you have interacted with over the past year and say, "If I have done anything this year to offend you, please forgive me." And if the person has done anything to offend you, you are to forgive that person as well. If the person refuses to forgive you, you are told to ask three times. If your third attempt is rejected, you are considered to be forgiven by God.

This practice needs to be done not just once a year but on a regular basis, especially with members of your family. There are many ways you may have offended or upset another person without being aware of it. It is important to become aware, acknowledge the wrongdoing, and seek forgiveness on the spot. Often just acknowledging an error and apologizing for it takes the sting away.

Forgiveness is a wonderful way of not only creating peace but also letting go of pride, which refuses to admit wrongdoing. Righteousness, defensiveness, arrogance, and pride are great enemies of peace. The simpler and more sensitive you become, the more you respect others and judge them favorably, the more you are keeping the true Torah and preventing harm from taking place. Nowhere is this more vividly manifested than in your relations with your family.

As you try to keep peace in the family and all your relationships, it is important to maintain open, ongoing communication with others. Unless you make it possible for others to tell you how they feel, without justifying yourself, blaming, or making them feel guilty, difficulties remain hidden and do not have the opportunity to get cleared away.

## The Zen Practice of Community: Sangha

The three pillars on which Zen practice is found, the three Zen treasures, are Buddha, dharma, and sangha. As mentioned, the sangha is the Zen community, those who sit, work, and sometimes live together, unifying their energies, giving and re-ceiving guidance, encouragement, and support.

Although you sit on your cushion alone and must face your life and death by yourself, it is a treasure to have other stu-dents sitting beside you, doing the same. Even when you sit alone, you are still sitting with a long stream of students, those who have taught you how to sit, those who have left their teachings behind, those in your life who have offered words of inspiration. It would be impossible to continue practice or even life without others. Ultimately, as practice deepens, the need arises to share, to express, and to offer the gifts you have received as well. You could not do that without others either.

Unlike your natural family, those who become dharma brothers and sisters (the sangha) appear in your life differently. You are drawn together by karmic propensities, and share a similar life direction. Sangha gathers together based on deep inner connections (that have been going on, perhaps, for many lifetimes). You join together for a purpose—to wake up, realize yourselves, and practice dharma together.

The sangha comes from all walks of life, all races, religions, conditions, and educational backgrounds. As you sit and prac-tice together, you forge a profound, timeless bond that tran-scends race, religion, or any other social classification. The feeling of oneness that grows among sangha members is differ-ent and sometimes deeper than that between those in a bio-logical family. We connect with one another on an intuitive basis, and after years of sitting together experience no separa-tion; wherever we go, we are at one. Of course, as in the fam-ily, problems arise in the sangha as well: conflict, upset, misunderstanding, hard times. Not only is this natural, it is inevitable. Problems are the fuel for practice and are to be used as an aid to growth. As you have difficulty with others, you cannot avoid seeing the parts of yourself that need to be worked with, parts that may be greedy, withholding, demanding, unforgiving or controlling. As you see these difficult aspects of yourself, you become able to let them go.

## Walking in the Footsteps of Peace

All of Zen is basically the practice of making peace—within ourselves, between one another, and in the world at large. The Zen direction, however, puts great emphasis on peace within. Unless we come to peace, acceptance, and wholeness within, we cannot find or provide peace in our relationships. And, the he way we are in relationships is a clear manifestation of the peace and unity we have found within. The modern-day Zen master Thich Nat Hahn describes this beautifully: "Although we cannot cover the entire world with peace, we can cover our own feet and, one step at a time, walk along, bringing peace with us."

If we try to fix a troubled world while we ourselves are filled with anger and confusion, we are of little value. Our ultimate contribution is who we are. We do not cover the truth of who we are with good intentions or the fight for causes. First we sit down on the cushion and face ourselves. When we are ready, we can bring true ease of heart wherever we go.

There are wonderful, specific steps Zen students take day in an day out to make peace within themselves and others. Along with zazen, *kinhin* (walking meditation), chanting, cleaning, cooking, eating, and sewing, there are guidelines for behavior in general and precepts (discussed above). Each of these precepts and guidelines is a form of practice, protection, mindfulness, loving care, and renunciation. You renounce your self-centered focus and choose to walk in the footsteps of peace, for your own sake and the sake of the world.

The following instructions for practicing peace can be applied to any situation. They interact beautifully with the mitzvot and in many ways complement them. These instructions have been given by the Buddha as well as many great Zen teachers. Basically, these steps ask you to renounce your negativity and self-centered obsession and devote yourself to the good of all.

### DO NOT LOOK AT THE FAULTS OF OTHERS

The Buddha gave a very great teaching for dealing with problems in the sangha, the family, and the world at large: "Do not look at the faults of others. Look at your own deeds, done and undone." This describes practice beautifully.

When you wish to create true and lasting peace, take your attention away from the external situation that is causing distress. Do not focus on fixing it or changing others, casting blame or condemning. Instead, take total responsibility for what is happening and look within. The only one you can change is yourself. As you follow this instruction, you examine your part in the situation. What have you done or left undone? Correcting your own part in it is the best way to alter a difficult situation.

## Lojong Teachings

The Lojong teachings are part of the Tibetan Buddhist scriptures. They include sayings to meditate on, to take with you in daily life, and to use as a reminder when faced with various situations. There are many wonderful Lojong teachings that offer guidance in making and keeping peace. Pema Chodron, a great Buddhist teacher and author, emphasizes these teachings and provides materials describing them. The ones cited below are described more fully in her book, *Start Where You Are.*

### "DRIVES ALL BLAME INTO ONE"

Everyone is looking for someone to blame. Instead, pause and look at what's happening within you. Lessen your own reactivity.

### DON'T WAIT IN AMBUSH

Don't wait for the moment when someone you don't like is weak to let him have it.

### DON'T MALIGN OTHERS

You may think speaking badly of others will make you feel superior. However, it only sows seeds of cruelty in your heart and causes others to mistrust you.

### DON'T TALK ABOUT INJURED LIMBS

Don't build yourself up by talking about other people's defects.

### DON'T TRANSFER THE OX'S LOAD TO THE COW

Don't transfer your load to someone else. Take responsibility for what is yours.

### DON'T ACT WITH A TWIST

Don't act with an ulterior motive of benefiting yourself. It's sneaky.

## DON'T BRING THINGS TO A PAINFUL POINT
Don't humiliate others.

### SENDING AND TAKING

The Tonglen teachings are a foundational practice in Tibetan Buddhism. Pema Chodron describes and utilizes them extensively, as do many other Tibetan masters. They are powerful in erasing negativity and producing good will. Though they may sound daunting at first, once you get used to them, they are natural, joyful, and easy to do. Pema Chodron describes this practice succinctly. "Whatever pain you feel in a situation, take it in, wishing for all beings to be free of it. Whatever pleasure you feel, send it out to others. In this way our personal problems and delights become a stepping-stone for understanding the suffering and happiness of all beings." When you are in a painful situation, imagine the pain to be a dark cloud and breathe it in. Then, imagine the dark cloud within transforming into light and breathe out the light and love to the people involved and the situation.

This may seem counterintuitive to the way you normally respond. Usually when people are involved in a conflict, they wish to win, to obtain good results for themselves only. If you wish to break through this negative state of mind, do the reverse. No matter how you are feeling, send light and love to all, including yourself and your own painful feelings. You do not have to actually experience a feeling of love, just intend it and say within, "I send you light and love." Even if you cannot take in negativity, you can still send forth light and love. There are other aspects of the practice, but this is the core. It immediately alters the energies present and softens and opens your own heart as well.

### THROWING STRAW ON MUD

Another wonderful description of how to make peace is offered by the great Vietnamese Zen Master Thich Nat Hahn, who teaches engaged Buddhism. He describes the ways in which monks at a monastery deal with conflict in their sangha. There are seven steps or principles in it, which lead to healing and reconciliation. This process can be applied to everyone everywhere. It is beautiful and effective.

### FACE-TO-FACE SITTING

The entire community sits on cushions, face-to-face. The two opposing monks are present and are aware of the fact that everyone expects them to make peace. This overall expectation is crucial. It is agreed in advance that the two monks will accept whatever verdict is pronounced by the whole assembly, or they will have to leave the community.

### REMEMBRANCE

All remember their purpose and what they are here for. In particular, they are now here to mend things of the past.

### NONSTUBBORNNESS

All agree to be open and not cling to a one-sided point of view. Each person has his own experience, which is to be respected. When we cling to a fixed view, we cut out the other and limit what is possible. Ultimately the outcome is less important than the process itself, which is healing. Each monk does his best to show his willingness for reconciliation and understanding. In this step alone, he is offering forgiveness and also forgiving himself.

## COVERING MUD WITH STRAW

The mud is the dispute and the straw is the lovingkindness of the dharma. Whatever happened will be met with warmth, compassion, and lovingkindness. This permits the exploration and reconciliation to take place.

## VOLUNTARY CONFESSION

Each monk reveals his own shortcomings, without waiting for others to say them. He tells what he did wrong in the situation. This deescalates the conflict and permits mutual understanding and acceptance. Each monk sacrifices his ego and his false image of himself. He stands in the shoes of the other and takes a larger view of himself.

## DECISION BY CONSENSUS

The outcome is decided by consensus and the monks accept the verdict.

## CREATING A SUPPLE, PEACEFUL MIND

Many of the basic principles of Zen practice lead to a mind that is inherently peaceful and flexible, with no room for conflict to fester and grow. Some of the principles are listed below.

## OPENNESS

Suffering is created by fanaticism and intolerance. Remain open to all views, but do not be bound by any of them. Human life is more important than any ideology or doctrine. All life is precious and must be carefully nurtured. Peace is lost through all forms of fanaticism.

## FREEDOM FROM
## IMPOSING OUR VIEWS

Trying to impose your views on others causes a great deal of suffering. Therefore, do not try to force anyone to adopt your views, even your children. Instead, respect the right of others to be different, to choose what to believe.

## OPEN, HONEST
## COMMUNICATION

Lack of communication always brings suffering and separation. You should commit to practice compassionate listening and loving speech and make every effort to keep communication open and reconcile all conflicts.

## TRUTHFUL
## AND LOVING SPEECH

Commit to speaking truthfully and constructively, using words that inspire hope and confidence.

## PROTECTING THE SANGHA

Never use the sangha for personal gain or profit.

## DWELLING IN
## THE PRESENT MOMENT

As life is available only in the present moment, commit to training yourself to live deeply each moment of daily life. Don't be carried away by regrets about the past, worries about the future, or cravings, anger, and jealousy. In this way you nourish seeds of openness and joy and share them with others.

# Guidelines to
# the Practice of Peace

## THE DYNAMICS OF FORGIVENESS

This can be practiced with anyone, whether in the family or not. The ongoing practice of forgiveness is fundamental for both peace with others and peace within.

### Step 1: Acknowledgment

Sit down and write about each member of your family, what you wanted from that person, how you wanted he or she to be.

Acknowledge each member of the family for who they were.

Allow all family members to be exactly who they are. Realize that who they are is not a reflection on you.

Describe how you were in the family.

Allow yourself also to be exactly as you were, no matter what others felt about you.

Describe what each family member gave you and the ways in which they supported your life.

Describe what you gave them.

### Step 2: Giving Thanks

Write a thank-you letter to each member of the family for something important you received from him or her.

Are there any gifts you may want to give these family members? Give one today.

There is no better way to practice forgiveness than to develop a grateful mind. Spend time each day being aware of what you have to be grateful for. Find ways to continually offer thanks.

### Step 3: Apologize

Rather than dwell on how family members hurt or disappointed you, look and see if there is something you need to apologize for. If there is, do it. Write a note of apology. Ask for forgiveness. Even if the offense took place a long time ago, this will be very healing for you. It will also mean a great deal to the other person.

Find out how you can make it up now. You can ask, or think of a way to make recompense. Now do it. If you cannot make recompense to a member of your own family, perhaps you can do this with someone else.

### Step 4: Start Anew

Describe your highest values for how a family can be. What is it you want to experience in your family? Do all you can to create this now. If you cannot do it with your given family, choose friends and create relationships that reflect these values as well.

### NAIKAN

Naikan is a process that was developed in Japan and brought to this country by David Reynolds. It is a simple yet powerful exercise for making peace. There are three steps in each naikan sitting, which may last thirty to forty minutes.

*Step 1:* Carefully and specifically write down all you have received today.

*Step 2:* Carefully and specifically write down all you have given today.

Step 3: Carefully and specifically write down all the pain or harm you've caused today.

These three steps help you rebalance your heart, mind, and activities. Usually you spend your time thinking about how much you are giving and how little you receive. You do not notice or take in the endless gifts you receive daily. You also spend a great deal of time thinking of the wrongs others have done to you and are seldom aware of the ways in which you may be hurting or troubling another. This exercise balance that all out.

The third step is not intended to create guilt but to make you more sensitive and aware of your actions and their consequences. When you realize that you have hurt another, do not linger in guilt about it but simply correct your actions, offering a new response.

This exercise is to be done every day. Do naikan on the day. You can also do naikan on a relationship, dealing with three years of the relationship at each sitting. When you do it on a relationship, simply ask yourself (1) What did I give the person? ( 2) What did I receive from the person? (3) What trouble or pain did I cause the person?

This simple daily exercise can turn your life around in truly startling ways.

# CHAPTER 11

# Healing Sorrow: Tikkun Olam and Total Acceptance

*The whole world is medicine*
*What is the illness?*
— ZEN KOAN

THE QUESTION OF HUMAN suffering, its causes and cures, has occupied mankind throughout the generations. Endless ways of warding off pain and inviting good fortune have been devised, and yet to this day, the entire world is filled with suffering and conflict of all kinds. Joyful times are often short-lived, while periods of strife last longer. Although most strive relentlessly for happiness, the shadow of sorrow follows close behind. In order to keep hard times to a minimum, many restrict their lives and relationships. Others live with catastrophic expectations and cannot relax and enjoy the good that comes to them. Particularly today given the global unrest and our constant awareness of it, generalized fear and insecurity the entire world.

The ultimate goal of both Jewish and Zen practice is to heal suffering and create a life of peace, love, and joy. Although each practice offers somewhat different vantage points, both agree that in order to attain true healing and well-being, the real nature of suffering must be understood. What is it that actually causes our anguish? What is the root of pain? Once a diagnosis is made, the steps to cure are not far behind.

The Buddha said that all life is suffering. This statement has been thought to be a negation of life. But this is a misunderstanding. It is meant to suggest that when we understand the true causes of suffering, we have the possibility of ending it once and for all. In other words, the way we experience life itself is the basic cause of our distress.

When the Buddha was asked who he was, he said he was a physician who had come to cure the ills of the world. We have all been shot with a poison arrow and it was his job to pull the arrow out. It was not his job to analyze the arrow, discover how long or short it was, or at what angle it had pierced the subject. He simply had to pull it out as quickly as possible. Time was of the essence. What is this arrow? What is the poison the Buddha speaks of? Exactly how have we been shot?

From the Zen point of view, there are three poisons that afflict human life—greed, anger, and delusion (or ignorance). These afflictions differ in intensity as they affect various individuals and are created by karma—by our thoughts, words, and actions—in this lifetime and others. Life as we now know it is the inevitable result of the accumulation of the seeds we have planted. Sooner or later every seed must sprout, bringing its consequences. Suffering is caused by the many seeds planted, knowingly and unknowingly, at different times. Another way of saying this is that you reap what you sow. Although you may not know the original cause, you now experience its consequence.

Usually when we suffer, we look around for someone to help or save us from what we're going through. During illness, we expect the doctor to take control of the disease and make us well again. But from the Zen point of view this attitude is part of the original disease. Behaving in this manner, you relinquish your part in the illness and deny that it has come to you for a reason. It's up to you to stop, listen, and discover the meaning and the lessons it brings. If you have created your karma, you can dissolve it as well. You can recognize it for what it is, take appropriate actions, and plant new seeds for the future; you are not the *victim* of the world you experience. Once you learn the lessons your suffering teaches and make efforts to turn it around, you become balanced and grow. This is the process of purification.

The process of purification heals illness of all kinds, physical, mental, emotional, spiritual. Both Zen and Jewish practice offer practices of purification. These practices are to be done daily, and there are also special seasons and occasions when the individual leaves his usual routines and focuses upon purification more intensively.

## The Jewish Practice of Healing the World: Tikkun Olam

Jewish practice is based on tikkun olam, discussed in Chapter 6. This means to heal, balance, and correct the world. "Tikkun" also means fixing (another word for purification). The Torah teaches that not only do we have to fix (balance) ourselves, but ultimately it is our responsibility to fix and heal the entire world. When we experience sorrow, loss, and suffering, it is so that we can learn to rectify the difficulty, heal the pain, and bring more light to both ourselves and others. The suffering we experience is basically a fire that purifies and balances our souls.

Jewish practice focuses on the fact that world healing cannot take place without each one of us. Even the smallest action, taken at the proper time in the proper way, has a huge effect not only on the person who performs it but on many worlds—minerals, vegetables, animals, humans, angels, and the world of those who have passed away. You are part of a huge, interlinked system and every word you speak, thought you think, and action you perform either helps heal the world or tear it down. To think that your life is meaningless and random or that what you do is of no importance is a dangerous delusion that contributes significantly to the suffering you undergo by creating the experience of meaninglessness.

The sense that the world is chaotic, exists at the mercy of random possibilities, and is not governed by God or higher intelligence, leads to the experience of *keri*, or meaninglessness. This condition of despair is called thrownness by existentialists. The experience of thrownness tells us that we have appeared out of nowhere, have been thrown into life at the mercy of forces we cannot govern. We are basically powerless; we suffer greatly and then disappear into an empty void.

From the Jewish point of view, the experience of thrownness, or meaninglessness, is the fundamental cause of all suffering. Without knowledge of and a way to connect to God, your greatest need—to know and live your life's purpose—is destroyed. Torah teaches that the way to overcome this darkness is to connect with God, over and over again. The entire world can become a veil, confusing you about your true purpose and creating a sense of being separate and alone.

Torah teaches that the experience of meaninglessness comes from the dark side (*sitra achra*), the side of confusion. Interestingly enough, these dark forces (sin and evil) have no inherent power. They exist only to strengthen you as you struggle with choices you have to make. Your ultimate protection and victory comes from your choice to do mitzvot, study Torah, and be connected to God. When you choose this, you remove yourself from dark forces and transmute them into light.

The truth of this is particularly heightened during times of distress. When an individual falls ill or is trapped in painful circumstances, his ability to deal with these difficulties is greatly strengthened when he senses a larger meaning as to why this is taking place and does not see himself as a helpless victim.

## Choose Life

The ability to choose is a profound aspect of Jewish practice, and a great human gift. Whatever happens in your life is given to you so that you may have an opportunity to choose. All day long you are presented with choices which will either lead to growth and joy or to destruction and sorrow. In this context it is important to note that the word "sin" means error, means missing the mark, or making a wrong choice. When you sin, you have simply made a wrong choice and may correct it at any time. Your very ability to make choices is an integral part of your deepest healing.

The Lubavitch Rebbe teaches that we are free to choose either good or evil and our choice has momentous consequences for ourselves and for the entire world. The very existence of evil, of—suffering, conflict, pain, and darkness—exists so that we can choose. This choice is not necessarily easy. We are often drawn to that which is not good for us; we crave pleasure and run from pain. Often we don't know the difference between them. In order to break free of this confusion, a struggle is needed. This struggle is necessary and positive. It makes us strong and provides energy to prevail. When we choose good and seek to fulfill our true mission, divine assistance is always at hand.

## The Zen Practice of Not Choosing

Zen offers a different view of illness and suffering. It does not speak about separation from God, but separation from ourselves and from truth. We get sick because we act in sickening ways. We are false to others and to ourselves and live searching for temporary pleasures to numb our pain Living this way we are tossed about like puppets, thrown about on the waves of change.

## Do Not Separate What You Like from What You Dislike

Sosan, a great Zen Master, offers a simple and direct medicine to cure suffering: "Do not separate what you like from what you dislike." Do not choose this or that. Do not accept what you love or reject what you hate. Don't make this kind of division. By dividing the world into good and bad, you are creating schism, duality, and discord; you are pulling life apart.

Usually we spend our precious energy either searching for and clinging to what we love, or running from and rejecting what we hate. In this way, we cling to half of our experience, labeling it good, and live in fear of losing it. We discard the other half of our experience, labeling it bad, and living in fear of attracting it.

The problem is further compounded when we identify with external circumstances. When "good" things happen, we feel proud and worthwhile; when "bad" things happen, we feel as though we've failed or are being punished. Our sense of who we are becomes dependent on passing events. As conditions change all the time this keeps us on an endless merry-go-round, where we can never win. Somehow we are not willing to just accept and experience each moment of life as it is.

The dualistic mind is the mind that separates. It is run by rigid ideas, focuses on differences, labels each experience and person and compares it with the next. Nothing is permitted to be what it is. Whatever we experience through the dualistic mind ultimately produces suffering. The dualistic mind removes us from our direct, whole, and utterly satisfying contact with life as it is.

## Learning to
## Live with Change

The dualistic mind hides the important fact from us that all experiences change and fluctuate. They cannot do otherwise. This is the law of transience. You cannot truly hold on to anything, including a fiction of who you are. When you live your life either grasping for the good or recoiling from the bad, you can never find true balance or respite from suffering.

A man was suspended over a cliff holding on to a tree branch for his life. Below him he saw a cavern where growling tigers were ready to eat him. His strength was giving out, and he could not cling to the branch forever. With his last bit of energy, he used his lips to pull a a strawberry off the branch and ate it. "How delicious," he said.

Like this man, Zen teaches that we are all suspended over the cavern of time, slowly facing the moment when we will let go of the branch that connects us to life. While we are still here, can we find the strawberry delicious and thoroughly enjoy it? When we can, our suffering ends.

This does not mean that we do not feel pain at times, but pain and suffering are different. Pain is inherent in many situations and cannot be avoided. Suffering comes from fighting a situation, and adding all kinds of painful interpretations. When you fully accept the situation and the pain, it does not turn into suffering. In order to pull out the poison arrow of suffering, you must learn to stand full square in the center of your experience and fully taste each moment for what it is.

## Ways of Healing Suffering

Both Zen and Jewish practice provide ways to interrupt our patterns and routines, change our focus, and go deeper into the essential truths of our lives. Both practices include times and seasons when we are asked to withdraw from life as we know it, gather our scattered energies, let go of worldly concerns, and focus on healing, reflection, and unification. These are times when we are given the opportunity to step back, see more deeply, and return to our original selves. This is the way to heal suffering and become all we are meant to be. In Zen practice, these periods of deeper reflection are called sesshin; in Jewish practice, they are called the *chaggim*, the holidays and festivals.

## The Zen Practice of Sesshin

Sesshins are periods of intensive practice when you are giving the opportunity to devote yourself entirely to practice. A sesshin that can last from one to ten days or longer. Once sesshin starts, no one can leave. Although there are different schedules at different Zen centers, the day usually begins at four in the morning and does not end until nine or ten at night. During sesshin you keep silence, do zazen, chant, clean, eat your meals in zazen posture, listen to a talk by the Zen master (teisho) daily, and have a daily meeting (dokusan) with him or her.

Sesshin is a time when you must face yourself in all respects. Distractions and toys are taken away, and activities are carefully scheduled. Whether or not you feel like it, you must attend everything. Although you do not speak or interact with others, you strongly feel the support and strength the sangha provides. As you sit in the silence, you go through everything—times of pain, joy, fear, peace, happiness, loss, gain, confusion, and understanding. During this time you have an opportunity to contact your inner strength, determination, and ability to persevere. Sesshin is a time of purification. By not running away, you become able to see the true nature of suffering and how it naturally fades away.

During one sesshin I attended when I first started to practice Zen, we came to the evening of the third day, when we had been sitting in zazen for seventeen hours a day. At this point, I had developed almost unbearable pain; I was exhausted and wanted to go home. My legs were aching and my back was stiff. I couldn't stand the thought of sitting for another second, but it was time for the evening period to begin. People were filing in and sitting down on their cushions. They all looked fine. What was wrong with me? Three more hours to go. I didn't think I could make it.

I sat down on my cushion and listened to the bells ring out. Then, absolute silence. Soon the pain began to mount. There was no way I could escape it. The more I fought it, the worse it became. Finally I broke the silence and started sobbing. I knew I was disturbing others, but I couldn't stop. The more I cried, the worse I felt.

Then, to my horror, Dogo, the head monk shouted at me loudly, "Eshin, shut up or get out. If you don't stop crying, you'll have to go sit by yourself down at the lake. There is no pain. You are the pain. Become stronger than the pain."

At that moment I stopped struggling. The pain went. Instead there was incredible joy. Sesshin is great medicine for sorrow. You heal your sorrow by entering it 100 percent. As you do so, you see that sorrow and joy are simply two sides of one hand and you do not give either of them the ability to derail your life. When you live in this manner, compassion develops toward everything you encounter and your actions naturally bring benefit and avoid harm.

## The Jewish Practice of Festivals

In Jewish practice, suffering is addressed and healed through prayer, study, relationship, and joy. Intensive times of practice, called the festivals, or *chaggim*, are devoted to this. They are like Jewish sesshins. Holidays and festivals take place regularly throughout the year, and intensively for one month during the Jewish New Year. During this period there are many days when work and life as usual come to a halt. All go to synagogue to pray, study, sing, dance, eat, and give honor to God. The festivals are known as times of rejoicing, times of deep thanksgiving and celebrating aspects of life.

The different Jewish holidays and festivals play a crucial part in the general tikkun or fixing of a person, a family, a community, and the world. It is said that divine energies are drawn down during this period to assist, cleanse, and bless everyone. Each festival hallows and corrects something that is out of balance, and addresses different aspects of a person's life. Each festival also brings special teachings and inner qualities to be developed. Inevitably, it also brings challenges and tests.

On all of the holidays and festivals Jews are called on to share deeply with others, open their doors, and let those who are hungry come and eat. This refers to all kinds of hunger, emotional, material, psychological, and spiritual; not just hunger for food. During the festivals all are included, everyone's home and heart are to be open wide.

### Times of Rejoicing

"It is a positive commandment to be happy during the festivals," Torah says. In Judaism the highest service to God is given through joy and happiness, praise and thanks. All sadness and suffering comes from a lack of appreciation of the great gifts we have been given and are being given daily. The festivals turn this around. We are constantly made aware of all the gifts of life, surrounded by friends, family, loved ones, delicious food, beautiful clothes, and joy. To fulfill the mitzvah of being happy on the holiday we eat wonderful meals, drink wine, wear festive clothing, and experience delight. A man is obligated to make his wife happy with lovely clothes (and in other ways), and to give sweets to his household. The happiness that a person has in doing a mitzvah is considered a service to God. This happiness itself is a healing from sorrow. Ultimately the festivals turn sorrow into joy.

## Year After Year

These festivals are observed season after season, year after year. Although the festivals are the same each year, year after year our circumstances differ. Some years the festivals are difficult to observe, other years easy and joyous. It can be hard to deal with the intense memories that arise, to be acutely reminded of the passage of time and people who have departed. Nevertheless, we are called on to remember and pray for them all. As we do so, we cannot help but see ourselves from the perspective of the generations. We must always remember what is expected of us, the heights to which we are called.

## Participate Fully

Like sesshin, Jewish festivals demand participation, an essential ingredient in healing sorrow. For this reason, a Jew is not permitted to leave the community during festivals. The festivals are communal gatherings; you may not absent yourself, cannot hide and wallow in private sorrow. You must stand up, offer yourself, and participate with all. As you do so, you realize you have a great deal to offer; your presence relieves the suffering of others, as well as your own.

Each holiday and festival focuses on a different theme, addresses a different form of suffering or imbalance. There are many major and minor holidays, festivals and times of observance. To go into all of them is beyond the scope of this book. The following is a brief overview of some of the major ones, the issues they address, and the healing they provide.

## Rosh Hashanah: Time of Teshuvah— Repentance and Return

The Jewish New Year is a time when both Jews and the entire world are given an opportunity to renew themselves. God says, "Return to me and I will return to you." Rosh Hashanah is a time of teshuvah, which means both repentance and return. You return to God, to yourself, and to the meaning of your life. In some places the shofar, ram's horn, is blown every day during the month preceding the holiday in preparation, to awaken the soul and cause it to return. During the holiday itself, the shofar is blown many times.

Rosh Hashanah is considered the coronation of the King. During this period, we renew our relationship to God and make him king over our lives. It is also a period of judgment and deep introspection. Many practices are involved with Rosh Hashanah. The entire month that precedes it, Elul, is considered a time of preparation. You make a careful accounting of the year before, how you have and have not behaved, and where you are now. It is said that special energy is available during this period to correct wrongdoing, look deeply within, and start anew. You express regret for errors and vow not to repeat them. Complete repentance (correction) comes when an opportunity arises to repeat the same error, and you refrain. All through this period you pray for help, pray for others, ask for forgiveness, and focus intensively on doing mitzvot. As you do this, you are returning to your Source.

Teshuvah, or return, is such an important practice in the healing of sorrow that it is helpful to look at it more closely. The letters of the word teshuvah allude to five paths of repentance, or return:

- T—Be sincere with God: "You found his heart faithful before you."

- Sh—Keep God before you constantly: "I have set HaShem before me always."

- U—Repentance must come from a good heart: "Love your fellow as yourself."

- V—See divine providence working: "In all your ways know him."

- H—Dispel arrogance: "Walk humbly with your God."

The Torah states the process succinctly: "What I ask of you is to do kindness, love justice, and walk humbly with your God."

## Yom Kippur: Day of Atonement

Yom Kippur, which comes about a week after Rosh Hashanah, is considered the holiest day of the year. It is a day of ultimate purification, based on forgiveness. In preparation you are to contact those you have interacted with in the previous year and ask for forgiveness. From sundown the night before to sundown of the next day you fast and pray for forgiveness and must extend forgiveness as well. At the end of the day, the judgment is completed. It is constantly emphasized throughout both Yom Kippur and Rosh Hashanah that prayer, charity, and mitzvot cancel a stern decree.

Right after the fast ends, observant Jews immediately start building their sukkah (outdoor hut) in preparation for Sukkot, which comes seven days later.

## Sukkot: Festival of Booths

Sukkot, or the festival of booths, is a time of harvest, great rejoicing, and fulfillment. Historically, Sukkot was the time when the crops were taken in. However, once again, Jewish practice interweaves the physical and spiritual, and the festival comes to remind us that our sustenance does not come from the earth, but from God who rules nature.

During Sukkot, Jews are told to leave their homes and dwell in booths for seven days. You leave your possessions and build a fragile, temporary dwelling place with a leafy roof through which you can see the sky. Many specific details are given about how to build this dwelling. As you build and live in the sukkah, you are reminded that life on earth is fragile and temporary, and that your body, like the sukkah, can blow away at any time. This is a time to give up clinging to the physical world and completely rely on God. It is also a time to welcome guests into your sukkah. There are many sukkah parties where all rejoice at the blessings of life, protection, friendship, and abundance.

One of the main mitzvot of Sukkot is to take four species—a lulav (palm branch), esrog (large lemon-like fruit), myrtle, and hyssop—and bind them together and shake them in specified ways. This has many deep meanings, among them banishing darkness, being victorious, and uniting all people and aspects of life.

When my grandfather came home from synagogue, walking down the street with the lulav in his hands, his eyes were shining so brightly that you could see him for blocks away. He laughed and greeted children as he walked, placing his hands on their heads. When he put his hands on my head, I felt streams of light pouring through, like a river that had no end.

His sukkah was in the garden behind our house, near grapevines. My grandfather ate, prayed, studied, sang, received guests, and slept in the sukkah for a whole weeklong. The only time he left it was to go to synagogue. I sat at his side the whole time, and as I did, it became very clear that no matter where else we might ever be, this fragile sukkah was our true home.

The end of Sukkot is a mystical time, Shemini Yitzeris, when those who have passed away come close to earth. Before you return to life as usual, God asks you to linger with him one more day. When Shemini Yitzeris ends, all gather together to sing and dance and rejoice with the Torah during Simchah Torah.

## Passover: Exodus from Slavery to Freedom

Passover is the festival of freedom that always occurs in the spring, though a different time each year, depending on the

Hebrew calendar. This festival is central to Jewish observance. The Torah says, "In every generation and every day, a Jew must see himself as if he had been liberated from Egypt that day." This is a way of remembering the great miracles that God performed and is still performing today. It is also a way of remembering the dangers of enslavement we all face daily.

Each year during Passover Jews receive a special opportunity to escape from everything that has bound and constricted them, to leave the pharaohs of their lives behind, the false, demanding, cruel authorities. All forms of leavening are removed from the home. During the week Jews eat only matzah. Leavening and the yeast that causes it to rise represent ego that which puffs you up and makes you proud. Like the matzah they eat, Jews are to become simple and plain, not puffed up and arrogant.

Each festival focuses on developing a different quality in the individual. Rosh Hashanah focuses on repentance, Yom Kippur on forgiveness. Passover is based on developing faith. Those who were taken from slavery only escaped due to their faith. (Many did not go.) The sea through which they fled to freedom did not actually part until they had the courage to walk in up to their necks. Their faith was being tested and had to be demonstrated before they could be free. As in days of old, our faith is constantly tested today. Are we willing to follow the word of God, go against the prevailing authorities, and travel to a place we know nothing of? Our unwillingness to do so is the cause of bondage. Our attachment to the status quo and our belief in our own weakness and limitations are heavy chains we all live with. During the exodus, these chains were broken.

## Shavuous: Receiving the Torah

The culmination of the exodus from Egypt, the escape from bondage to freedom, came when the Torah was received. Shavuous is the festival that commemorates the acceptance and receiving of the Torah. The sages say that the Torah is constantly being given and comes down anew every year on Shavuous. New revelations come into the world. Each year we have a new opportunity to accept the teachings and mitzvot as well. As part of preparation, many stay awake the night before studying and preparing themselves to receive the Torah.

## The Zen Practice of Freedom

Every time you sit in zazen, you are also engaged in the act of return; you turn around, face the wall, and return to yourself and your Source. In this process purification and repentance take place naturally. Then, when you get up from the cushion, another kind of return happens as well; you return to both everyday activities and to your relationships. In this turning and returning, you are constantly cleansed, tested, and taught to live in the fullest and purest way possible.

Zazen practice is also a purification. You look into and cleanse your heart and mind. In addition, every morning there is a verse of confession during morning service, which is preparation for not only for zazen but for the day: "All the evil karma ever committed by me since of old on account of my beginningless greed, anger, and folly, born of my body, mouth, and thought, I now confess and purify them all."

You do not repent or confess to others but look unremittingly into the depths of your own life and heart. As you sit and look within, you cannot hide from the truth of who you are and what has gone on. When remorse arises, it sears negativity away. By experiencing this deeply, when you get up from the sitting, your behavior naturally changes. The Zen view of repentance is interesting. The late Uchiyama Roshi, a modern-day Zen Master, said, "To truly repent does not mean offering an apology, repenting requires standing before the Absolute and letting the Absolute light illuminate us." The Samantabhada Sutra says, "If you wish to repent, sit zazen and contemplate the true nature of all things."

## Guidelines to Jewish Practice

### MAKING CORRECTIONS

What is it in your life that needs healing? Write it down.

Write down the ways in which you usually cope with it. Do they work?

Look within and see whether there is any wrongdoing or error in your life that you need to address. Write them down. Also write down ways in which they can be cleared up. Is an apology due? Do you need to accept an apology that has been given to you? Do you have to correct a lie? Do you respond harshly to insults?

Pick one issue and make the correction today.

Tomorrow do another one. As you keep this going, your suffering will diminish and you will find the taste of life and happiness returning to you.

### HEALING THROUGH JOY

What brings joy into your life? What are you willing to celebrate totally?

Take time to stop your usual activities, thoughts, and complaints and celebrate something that is meaningful to you. Dance, sing, play, learn, give gifts, plan surprises. Invite others to share this celebration with you. See how you can make them happy and watch your sorrow drift away.

If you are drawn to celebrate a Jewish holiday or festival, go to a synagogue you feel comfortable with and join in. Learn more about the holiday. Many classes are available online and in classrooms. Do as much as you can and focus on that which was beneficial. Remember, it is a time of joy.

There is a special magic about doing zazen in connection with and in honor of the Jewish holidays and festivals. It is very powerful to do zazen and then pray, study, sing, or join with others in a holiday meal. Everything is intensified and becomes hallowed.

## Guidelines to Zen Practice

### SAYING YES

Is there a situation you are involved in which is causing unhappiness that you are not able to work out?

Today, for a little while, accept the situation entirely as it is. Relinquish your demands about it, your claims that it be different. Try to find something meaningful or positive in the situation. Stop fighting and struggling. As you do this, see what happens to your pain. And, very often, you may also notice that when you stop pushing and pulling, things often begin to change all by themselves.

For today, rather than blame others for your difficulty or sorrow, see it as part of your karma that is rising now. Consider how the ways in which you've functioned may have brought this about. What are you doing now to keep the situation going? You may also consider how certain changes in your usual ways would be beneficial, for both this particular situation and your life in general.

If you are drawn to practice zazen, this is a good place to begin. Start sitting a little. Do as much as you can. If you are drawn to learn more or sit with others, find a Zen center that you feel comfortable with and join in.

CHAPTER 12

# Understanding Life Purpose: Caring for One Another and Bodhisattva Activity

ULTIMATELY, THE FRUIT OF both Zen and Jewish practice is kindness. In both practices a person does not choose the recipients of her kindness but extends it to everyone, including those feared or disliked; enemies, friends, families, acquaintances, animals, and even the animals of enemies. In both practices, there is never any excuse not to offer kindness. Zen and Jewish practice both deeply explore the question of what kindness truly is. Zen warns us against "idiot compassion," and Jewish practice prescribes specific acts of kindness we may never have been aware of before. Sometimes what seems to be cruel can ultimately be an act of kindness and vice versa. But the true measure of any practice and practitioner is how kind they are, and the ways in which their kindness is offered to others.

## The Jewish
## Practice of Kindness

In Jewish practice, acts of kindness are specifically commanded. These guidelines are valuable in human relations, which can be confusing and complex. It is easy to perform an action you think is positive but has unintended negative effects. Then there are other times when acts of kindness may be desperately needed, and you may not be aware of it. Some blind themselves to the suffering around them, feeling as though they have no idea how to help. However, as you engage in Jewish practice, you are instructed exactly what to do under all kinds of circumstances. No matter how you are feeling or how unaware you may be, as you take specific steps, your actions will inevitably be those of compassion and sensitivity.

One day I brought a friend to synagogue for the Sabbath. The friend was not involved in Jewish practice but had been ill and desired to come and pray. After the services, the congregation went downstairs for a meal. My friend sat down beside me and, hungry, began to eat before the blessings had been said. A woman sitting behind us became upset. "Don't you know you can't eat before the blessing?" she scolded my friend loudly and harshly.

My friend was shocked and embarrassed. "I don't know anything," she retorted, "except that I don't belong here with you."

"That's obvious," the woman snapped.

Horrified by what was going on, I desperately wanted to join in. However, at that painful moment, I suddenly decided to follow the law, which says, in situations like this, when anger erupts, it is best to hold your tongue.

It was harder for me to hold my tongue that it would have been to sit still in zazen for two straight hours. The fight ended, the meal was eaten, and I left with my friend. Though I apologized to her profusely, I didn't make a dent. She promptly went home. I didn't blame her.

I had been invited to another meal later in the afternoon. Crestfallen, I decided to attend. I went to the meal and sat down at a long table. To my shock, the woman who had started the fight came in and promptly sat down beside me. Everyone else at the table was warm, animated, and enjoying a lively conversation. At first I tried to ignore this woman and speak to the person on my other side. However, she would not be ignored. "I don't know what kind of people you're friends with," she said, "but I'll tell you this, I would never pray for your friend or for you."

I was stunned. I looked at the woman's face, which was tight with bitterness. Although I wanted to give her a piece of my mind, once again, it suddenly struck me to follow the law, and I continued to keep the silence. This gave the woman an opportunity to go on.

"Why should I pray for you?" the woman continued?" As I sat there silently, suddenly I felt the depth of the woman's sorrow and pain.

"I'll never pray for you," she repeated.

"Well, I'll pray for you," I said quietly.

The woman became pale. Then she looked down and started to cry. "I'm so sorry for everything," she said softly. "Tell your friend, I'm sorry, I'm sorry. What a horror I've become."

By keeping the law in this instance, staying silent despite a strong wish to respond, I gave this unexpected exchange and healing a chance to take place.

## How to Get from I to We

Much of the sorrow we experience in life comes through others, and healing comes in this way as well. A fundamental way to heal our sorrow is through the practice of kindness. Service and kindness to others heal all. When we look at relationships in this manner, then the ways in which we are hurt, disappointed, and betrayed by others become the stepping-stones for growth, opportunities to do a mitzvah and offer kindness in return.

When viewed in this manner, relationships become a form of meditation. It is our very purpose in being here. Some of the major laws and mitzvot related to the Jewish practice of kindness and making peace are examined in Chapters 3 and 10.

## The Zen Practice of Kindness

In Zen practice kindness emerges naturally from who we intrinsically are. The kindness is not formulated but arises spontaneously and is appropriate to the particular moment and situation.

A physician seeking truth traveled far to find a teacher. Finally he came upon a Zen Master living in a small hut on top of a far mountain. "Tell me the essence of Zen," the seeker pleaded.

"Go home and be kind to your patients," the Zen Master said. "That is Zen."

A fruit of Zen practice is called bodhisattva activity, or kindness to others. A bodhisattva is a person who has awakened however, instead of focusing exclusively on his own enlightenment or simply living in comfortable circumstances, he takes a vow to dedicate his life to helping others awaken as well. This is considered the ultimate kindness. The bodhisattva does this by offering wisdom, guidance, and teachings and by being a wonderful example of what practice is about. In one form or another, the bodhisattva vow is recited during services. It is a beautiful statement of practice and intent.

The vow is spoken in many different ways. The following expression of the bodhisattva's way is recited during the sesshins I attended for years. It is found in the sutra book of the Zen Studies Society.

When I, a student of dharma, look at the real form of the universe, all is the never failing manifestation of the mysterious truth of Tathagata In any event, in any moment and in any place none can be other than the marvelous revelation of its glorious light. This realization made our patriarchs and virtuous Zen Master extend tender care, with a worshiping heart, even to such beings as beasts and birds.

This teaches us that our daily food and drink, clothes and protections of life are the warm flesh and blood, the merciful incarnation of Buddha. Who can be ungrateful or not respectful even to senseless things, not to speak of man? Even though he may be a fool, be warm and compassionate towards him. If by chance he should turn against us and become a sworn enemy, and abuse and persecute us, we should sincerely bow down with humble language, in reverent belief that he is the merciful avatar of Buddha, who uses devices to emancipate us from sinful karma that has been produced and accumulated upon ourselves, by our own egoistic delusion and attachment through the countless cycles of *kalpa*.

Then in each moment's flash of our thought there will grow a lotus flower, and on each lotus flower will be revealed a Buddha. These Buddhas will glorify *Sukhavati*, the Pure Land, every moment and everywhere. May we extend this mind over all beings so that we and the world together may attain maturity in Buddha's wisdom.

## The Zen and Jewish Road
## to Who You Truly Are

In Zen the road that leads back to the center of our lives is called the road of no road, or the gateless gate. Though we take many steps on it, with each step we are right where we belong. We are not traveling to some final destination. All is revealed right here, right now.

Much of Zen practice ultimately leads to the realization that there is a greater power, the Tao, that moves, guides, and inspires our every breath and word. This power dissolves ego and brings kindness, simplicity, and rest. By practicing zazen, you allow the greater power within to guide all of your life.

Torah provides an ideal image, a prototype of the perfect person to aspire to be. Interestingly enough, however, there are no saints described in Torah. The gap between the ideal and the reality of human nature is always recognized. The greatest leaders in Torah are filled with human failings. Even the greatest prophets are shown grappling with conflict, anger, and sorrow. It is the struggle between the ideal and our human responses, emotions, and tendencies which strengthens and purifies us.

Zen practice does not set up a conflict between who you are and an ideal person you are to become. It maintains that suffering and unkindness arise precisely because we cling to unrealistic images of ourselves—either who we are or who we are to become—and are not in touch with our true identity. In order to discover and live from our essential truth and kindness, Zen removes all ideals and images and offers total acceptance of who we are now.

This total acceptance is not resignation. It is a way of removing self-hatred and delusion that prevent us from growing naturally. Ultimately, this is an act of great kindness. The road to our ultimate destination is not outside of ourselves. If we open our eyes and really look, we see that we are walking on it right now.

## Guidelines to Jewish Practice

Take some time to note the ways in which you are, and are not, kind to others.

Also note what you expect back from your acts of kindness. (Realize that if you are expecting something in return, this is not true kindness at all, but a form of barter.)

Write this all down. Make a list. Pay attention to what you are noting.

Turn to one of the mitzvot related to kindness (in Chapter 10) and try it on for a week. Don't tell anyone about it. Do it for its own sake.

Write down all that happens to you as you do this, within and without.

Next week, try another deed of kindness, or mitzvah.

In your daily life, become aware of the many opportunities to reach out, touch, and help. Are you refusing them? Can you accept more each day?

Can you view events that come to you as opportunities to help? Note which mitzvot you are being offered. See if you are willing to say yes.

Note how ego and a sense of self-importance diminish as your life revolves around caring for others and being kind.

You can also choose to learn more details about each mitzvah listed above, as well s many others. Consult books that describe the mitzvot. Choose others that may strike you. Or choose a mitzvah that you have difficulty with.

Be aware of how your feelings of kindness fluctuate. No matter what you are feeling, you can always choose to engage in actions that are positive, constructive, and kind.

## Guidelines to Zen Practice

Become a Zen fisherman. As mentioned in Chapter 8, a Zen fisherman is an individual whose practice is ripe. He has left the mountaintop and come into the marketplace with open handsto help. One of the beautiful aspects of the Zen fisherman is that he is perfectly ordinary. He blends in inconspicuously and gives himself completely to life as it arises.

Take a look and see the ways in which you desire attention and praise for your "good" deeds. How do you want others to see you? In what ways do you want others to feel that you are better than they are? This is actually an act of unkindness. Stop all of this for a day or two. Become inconspicuous. Practice good deeds anonymously. Give up any desire for a return.

They say that if you look for the Zen fisherman you cannot find him. He appears no different from any other person around, except that wherever he goes, withered trees start to bloom. There are many withered trees in our lives and also withered people. By letting go of pretensions and developing gentleness and wisdom, you, like the Zen fisherman, can offer strength and inspiration to whomever you pass by.

# COMBINING JEWISH
# AND ZEN PRACTICE

AFTER WE HAD BEEN sitting together for many years, one day my Japanese samurai Zen master turned to me and said, "After all these years of sitting with you, by now I have become a Jewish grandmother. But you have not become a samurai yet."

"Not yet," I murmured to myself, wondering if the day would ever come.

A great deal of time is needed to digest, absorb, and make all the teachings real in our lives. Therefore, as we come to the close of this book, we are really coming to the beginning. The image of a circle is widely used in Zen. It reminds us that the beginning and the end are indistinguishable and that life is a whole. In Judaism the Shema prayer is said daily, also proclaiming that God is one, life is one, the entire world is one family. Great patience is needed to realize and live this, in both practices. Neither offers a quick fix. After a student sits for thirty years in Zen, the masters then tell her to sit for another thirty years. This is not just a saying; it is a fact. Thirty more years are needed, and after that another thirty years. There is no end to the depth and simplicity we arrive at. Seeds take time to hibernate under the earth and then sprout into life when conditions are ripened. As we sit, we sow the seeds and care for the garden of our lives.

In Jewish practice as well, the mitzvot are done daily, weekly, yearly, season by season, year after year. Although the practices remain the same year by year, year by year we are different. We understand the teachings differently, realize truths we have not seen before, offer ourselves more wholeheartedly, and perhaps take on new actions.

Above all else, do not judge yourself or your practice. Times of difficulty, doubt, and estrangement are natural. They will pass. Times of joy, fulfillment, and understanding are also natural, and also fade away. No matter what is happening, as the Zen masters remind us, "Just march on."

In both practices, there are aspects you may dislike or find too hard to do, other aspects you may thoroughly enjoy. And these feelings too change or turn around over time. The late Zen master Uchiyama Roshi referred to our passing feelings as "the scenery of our life." He said it is like riding on a train and looking at fleeting scenery from the window. Ultimately, these passing feelings, the passing scenery, do not matter. Just do what you can, day by day, week by week, year by year. In Zen this is called "just chopping wood, just carrying water." Do what you can and learn from it; then do it again. Most importantly, do not judge, reject, or overly value yourself. You never really know the effects of your efforts, no matter how small. Just do what you do as well as you can, and let the consequences take care of themselves.

Practicing with others is a great support. In my view, it is almost impossible to carry on a lifelong practice alone. We need connection and feedback from others, and those we practice with become our teachers as well. Over the years I have learned so very much from sangha members. Having tea after zazen, another student will say something to me in passing that impacts strongly and helps. Cleaning in the kitchen together or cutting vegetables, I notice something about how another student works or lends a hand in a certain way. It moves my practice forward. When I am discouraged or tired sometimes, during the walking meditation between sittings, I glance at the face of another student who suddenly looks beautiful, different than she did when the sittings began. I am uplifted and inspired and walk along more easily. For my part, I encourage the practice of others by my presence, a smile, by listening to something they have to say, or offering a word of inspiration. Sangha members are a real treasure, as are the Jewish congregants who help you see who you really are in how you respond to them .

Today the United States has dozens of wonderful Zen centers, each offering individuals the opportunity to pursue the practice of zazen and integrate it into their daily lives. In some Zen centers many students become monks and nuns, and there may be an emphasis on monastic practice. Other Zen centers are more geared toward laypeople. As practice goes forward in different Zen centers, including at the one I trained at for years, changes take place. Needless to say, nothing stays the same. If you choose to go, it's important to check out each one for yourself, including its background and history.

There are also many different Jewish congregations in which Torah is followed, interpreted, and honored differently. In order to find your own way, visit the different congregations and see where you feel most at home and where there is the greatest possibility of growth and acceptance.

Practicing both Zen and Judaism has brought balance and richness, as well as struggle, to my life. But I cannot do otherwise. Zen practice allows me to love being alive, be centered, independent, and receive the Torah teachings more deeply. When I sit I am able to grapple with the Torah honestly, make the teachings my own, and work toward actualizing them in my daily life. Practicing both Zen and Judaism has brought depth to my prayers and experience of myself, and an ever-increasing willingness to give and serve. Jewish practice provides wisdom, a connection to God, a sense of roots, of the generations, and an exploration of what it means to be human, providing a broad context for my life. Perhaps because I am so engaged in both practices, I have been moved to create our Jewish Zen center, where we have the kindness, mindfulness, and simplicity of Zen, combined with the moving prayers, wisdom, mitzvot, and blessings of Judaism. Anyone who takes on both practices must be willing to stand on his or her own two feet and integrate the teachings. It is easier to take on a ready-made identity as a Jew or a Zen student, but this is impossible for those who wish to integrate the two practices. Ultimately, one must constantly be true to oneself.

To find out more about Jewish and Zen practice and what is available or to contact the author, write topspeaker@yahoo.com, or see http://www.jewishdharma.com or http://www.brendashoshanna.com.